The Little Dogs' Beauty Book

Deborah Wood

t.f.h.

T.F.H. Publications, Inc.

The Little Dogs' Beauty Book

Project Team
Editor: Heather Russell-Revesz
Copy Editor: Joann Woy
Design: Mary Ann Kahn

T.F.H. Publications
President/CEO: Glen S. Axelrod
Executive Vice President: Mark E. Johnson
Publisher: Christopher T. Reggio
Production Manager: Kathy Bontz

T.F.H. Publications, Inc.
One TFH Plaza
Third and Union Avenues
Neptune City, NJ 07753

06 07 08 09 10 1 3 5 7 9 8 6 4 2

Library of Congress Cataloging-in-Publication Data
Wood, Deborah, 1952-
  The little dogs' beauty book : pamper and primp your petite prince or princess / Deborah Wood.
p. cm.
Includes index.
ISBN 0-7938-0587-2 (alk. paper)
1. Dogs--Grooming. I. Wood, Deborah. II. Title.
SF427.5.W66 2006
636.7'0833--dc22
2005028447

This book has been published with the intent to provide accurate and authoritative information in regard to the subject matter within. While every precaution has been taken in preparation of this book, the author and publisher expressly disclaim responsibility for any errors, omissions, or adverse effects arising from the use or application of the information contained herein. The techniques and suggestions are used at the reader's discretion and are not to be considered a substitute for veterinary care. If you suspect a medical problem consult your veterinarian.

The Leader In Responsible Animal Care For Over 50 Years!™
www.tfhpublications.com

CENTRAL
Garden & Pet

Table of Contents

Section 1

Haute Dog Couture

Fashion is fun. Nowadays, your dog can look flirty or funky, flashy or fabulous. There are clothes and boots for your four-legged family member, and an overwhelming choice of collars and leashes. Never before in the history of dogdom have there been so many delightful choices to make on a shopping trip.

Fashion can also practical. If you spend time thinking about the best way to keep your short-haired dog warm, you'll find the right sweater or jacket. Or, if you take some time to consider the construction of a collar and leash, you'll make better choices.

The most important thing to remember is that fashion can be a form of bonding. One of the traits that humans share with their canine companions is that we both love attention. We enjoy fashion because it's interactive— wear a great pair of shoes or a gorgeous necklace, and people stop and talk about it. The same can be true for your fashionable little dog.

Have fun!

Chapter 1

The Well-Clothed Canine

A little dog named Bruiser helped change the face of American dogdom. The hit movie *Legally Blonde,* starring the charming Reese Witherspoon as a ditzy law student, featured a tiny Chihuahua named Bruiser. For dog lovers, Bruiser was the real star of the movie. He's the dog who showed America that pooches look great in pink.

The revolution had begun, and there was no turning back—especially for those of us with little dogs. The days of putting our dogs in schlocky acrylic sweaters were over. Today, top designers are making trendy, fashionable dog clothes. There's something for every dog—dresses and rainwear, real leather and faux fur, boots and hats. And that doesn't even take into account the explosion in the availability of totally cool leashes and collars.

Finally, we get to dress our "furkids" just as well as our friends dress their human kids. Luckily for little-dog lovers, the world of canine couture is just as varied as human clothing. You can buy a T-shirt, or you can buy a fantastic designer winter coat for your petite pet. You can spend hundreds of dollars on an outfit, or you can make it yourself from remnants at a vintage store.

Dressing your dog is fun, it's fashionable, and it's here to stay.

Reasons (Other than Fashion) to Dress Your Dog

Of course canine couture is fun, but sometimes clothes for your little dog are more than just a fashion statement—even silly T-shirts can have a serious function.

Warmth

Your slender, short-haired Italian Greyhound isn't designed for Northern winters. Short-coated small dogs need help keeping warm, even in moderate climates like the Pacific Northwest. If you're going to be outside in Maine in winter, it matters that your little guy is in a warm coat. Sure, it's fun if the outfit is adorable, but the bottom line is that your little dog needs help keeping warm.

Even long-coated little dogs can sometimes use some help. Pomeranians were bred down from real sled dogs, and they still have the thick winter fur to prove it. But, small animals lose their body heat much faster than big dogs do. While the full-sized Alaskan Malamute is often comfortable spending hours in the cold, your little sled-dog descendant isn't—he may need a coat or sweater.

Because warmth matters, you'll want to be sure that you find coats and sweaters that are well-designed and made from materials that actually help keep your little guy snug on a blustery day.

Worried Dogs

Lots of dogs worry. There's more to worry about when you only weigh 5 pounds (2.2 kg), and the cat is bigger than you are. If your little dog is a bit shy, or something of a nervous Nellie, dressing him in clothes can actually help relieve some of his anxiety.

Why? Having his body wrapped sends calming signals to your dog's nervous system. Just like newborn babies are tightly wrapped in their blankets to make them feel secure, simply putting a T-shirt, sweater, or dress on your dog can make him feel calmer, too. Even better if the T-shirt says something like "Stud Muffin" or "Talk to the Paw."

Dogs Like Attention, Too

When you're wearing a fabulous party dress, people come up and compliment you. After receiving such positive attention, you'd probably wag your tail (if you had a tail, that is). The truth is that all of us like attention when we're dressed up, and your dog is no exception. Most dogs love to interact with people, and clothes are conversation starters. If your little princess is wearing a pink terry hoodie and matching pink go-go boots, she'll have fun when people stop and tell her she's precious. If your little dude is wearing a Hawaiian shirt and tennis shoes, he'll have a ball with all the people who can't resist smiling at him and petting him.

Having fun with your little guy is always a good thing, and dressing up your pet in fabulous fashions is definitely a way for the two of you to meet new people.

Dressing Your Dog

The man and his Chihuahua had pretty much the whole dog show staring—and that's hard to do. People usually don't get too excited by a dog when a couple of thousand of them are sitting, standing, and sleeping all over the fairgrounds. But the sight was dramatic enough that even the veteran show people had never seen anything quite like it.

The man looked like a professional wrestler—a big, beefy guy with a bald head and Chinese lettering tattooed on his shaved scalp. I asked him what the Chinese letters meant, and he told me, "No neck." It was an apt description.

He carefully cradled his tiny Chihuahua in his arms as he watched the outdoor dog show. He obviously adored the dog, and the dog adored the big, kind man. When a breeze came up and the air grew chilly, he pulled a sweater out from his pocket to put on the dog.

A fabulous dress can help spark lots of positive attention for your little dog.

9

That's when the entertainment began. The Chihuahua bared his tiny teeth and growled with a ferocity that could be heard a dozen yards away. I looked carefully to see if the dog was in pain or afraid—but that wasn't the case. Clearly, the 5-pound (2.2 kg) dog was accustomed to being in charge of the man (who weighed closer to 250 pounds (113 kg)), and he was telling the guy to keep his mitts off. The gentle man ignored stares of the crowd, as well as the growls and snarls and snaps of the dog, and calmly put the sweater on his little buddy. When the sweater was in place, the little dog sighed contentedly and snuggled into the man's arms, happy for the warmth.

If you're struggling to get a sweater on your dog (and you aren't as tough as Mr. No Neck) try these tips:

- ❋ Practice getting clothes on and off at home, and give your dog treats when you do. Make dressing time a happy time.
- ❋ Be sure to always take your time (even if a whole dog show is staring at you!). If you inadvertently make your dog uncomfortable when you're getting him dressed, he will hate it more.
- ❋ Massage your dog regularly (more on that in the Spa Dog section). When he's used to being handled, getting dressed is less traumatic.
- ❋ Select clothes that are easy to get on and off. Rather than having to pull a sweater on or off, try to find clothing with Velcro closings or snaps. Some outfits have more generous arm holes. Selecting clothes for comfort is just as important as style.

Finding Fido's Fashion Sense

Fashion is all about personal style, and no one has more personal style than your dog. Since you know your little guy better than anyone, take his personality into account when deciding what he should wear.

The Metrosexual Male

When most people think of dressing their dogs, they think of frilly pink bows and dresses. These types of outfits will just

Male dogs can have fun with fashion too!

not do for the cool metrosexual male dog. Sure, he wants to look great, and he has a wonderful sense of style, but he doesn't want to look like a pretty princess. Happily, now there are lots of clothing choices for your little male dog. He no longer has to look like a babe—so don't make him.

Here's a sampling of some male dog personalities, and some ideas for what each of them might want to wear.

The Alpha Male

This guy would be President if he had a chance (and opposable thumbs). Think Arnold Schwarzenegger or Bill Clinton. This isn't about size and muscle, it's about charisma—a larger-than-life personality who waltzes into a room. Men want to be his friend, and women find him charming.

The alpha male can wear anything; he likes campaigning and being the center of attention. Give him a fun T-shirt or even a hat—just don't make him wear pink.

The alpha male can wear anything.

The Protector

The Protector is the ultimate "Man" dog, even if he lives in the body of a Chihuahua. The protector lets you know who's at the door, and he'd lay down his life to protect you. Some protectors have a sweet side, too. They'll lend their favorite toy to your cat if she's feeling woozy from surgery. Dress the protector in finely made, but simple clothes—he needs to protect his serious image.

The Surfer Dude

My dogs have a friend we call Lucky Eddie. Eddie is a typical "dude"—laid back and friendly. He'll give you his bone if you ask for it. He's gentle with littler dogs, and avoids the tough dogs at the dog park. Eddie (and dogs with the same "hang loose" personality) looks great in a Hawaiian shirt. Cowabunga, dude!

The Scamp

This little guy is looking for a good time. His only regret is that you need to be 21 to get into the best clubs. This dog wants the attention, so the sky's the limit when deciding what to dress him in. But do make sure he's always on a sturdy (and fashionable) leash, because he'll be off in a flash, chasing cats, squirrels, or that adorable Toy Poodle down the street.

The Femme Fatale

Just like your metrosexual male, your little girl has her own personality type. She can run the gamut from sweet and demure to powerful and demanding. Luckily, there are clothes to match her every whim!

The Princess

The Princess is a girly-girl. Somehow, she manages stays tidy even when she plays at the beach. She likes to wear clothes that show off her adorable eyes and fabulous fur. Dress your Princess in anything pink, and anything with a heart-shape or butterfly—think Paris Hilton in a dog suit.

Dress your princess in anything pink.

Too Precious???

I'll never forget meeting Precious. He was an adorable Toy Poodle, whose doting mom had dressed him in a pink bow and painted his toenails a matching pink. I swear the dog was mouthing the word "Help" to me. Precious was actually a tough, friendly, masculine dog who would have looked great in a sweater or maybe a leather jacket. Dress your dog in something appropriate to his personality, and you'll have a happy little dog.

The Diva

The Diva is the dog in charge. She wants things her way, and she'll let you know when you're doing things wrong. An "Alpha Bitch" T-shirt—or better yet, a collar with real jewels—is always appropriate for the Diva.

I know a great Diva dog at the LexiDog Boutique & Social Club in Portland, Oregon. This specialty shop is the realm of a Miniature Pinscher named Lexi. A queenly portrait hangs over the office—a true Diva sneering down on her lowly subjects.

The Earth Mother

This little lady is dedicated to taking care of everything and everyone. She's a friend to all: The Princess and the Diva appreciate her steadiness, and puppies know she's a safe haven in any storm. Buy this dog something elegant but simple—you just know she'd never spend that money on herself!

The Tomboy

This sassy lassie likes action. She runs the agility course in no time flat, and plays with the boys at doggie day care. She wants clothes that allow her to move, move, move! Plenty of cute sporty clothes are available that can take lots of rough-housing and still look good.

What Color Is Your Little Dog?

Did you ever wonder why Yorkies look good in red, and a blonde Chihuahua is pretty in pink? Color analysis is the answer.

Color analysis took the human fashion world by storm during the past decade. It's hard to remember a time when people didn't say, "I'm an Autumn" or "I'm a Winter."

The concept is simple: The color of our hair and skin determines what clothes look best on us. Our palettes are divided into Summer, Winter, Spring, and Autumn. For example, I'm a classic Summer, with blonde hair and light eyes. I look jaundiced if I wear orange, but pink makes my skin look healthy and my eyes shiny. My little Papillon, Goldie, is an Autumn, with her copper-colored (and white) fur and dark brown eyes.

What color is your dog? Here's a summary of the color chart by season.

Autumn

Hair: golden brown, red, auburn or chestnut

Eyes: dark brown, hazel, or dark green

Typical breeds: Brussels Griffons, Pomeranians, Cavalier King Charles Spaniels, Papillons

The Autumn palette includes:

※ Neutrals: off whites, warm beiges, warm browns from light to dark, camel, gold

※ Mustard, pumpkin, terra cotta, rust, peach, and salmon

※ Orange, orange-red, tomato red

※ Lime green, yellow-green, moss green, grayed green, olive green, jade green, forest green

※ Turquoise, teal blue, dark periwinkle blue

※ Jewelry: gold

Every dog looks good in black.

Winter

Hair: black, ash black, brown

Eyes: blue, brown, hazel, or green

Typical breeds: Affenpinschers, Scotties, Yorkies, Poodles, Min Pins

The Winter palette includes:

- ❋ Neutrals: white, light grays to charcoal gray, black, taupe, navy
- ❋ True blue, royal blue, turquoise, royal purple
- ❋ True green, emerald green, pine green
- ❋ Hot pink, magenta, fuchsia, burgundy, blue-red, and true red
- ❋ Icy green, icy yellow, icy aqua, icy violet, icy pink, icy blue
- ❋ Jewelry: silver

Spring

Hair: golden blonde, golden brown, or red

Eyes: blue, blue-gray, blue green, or light turquoise green

Typical breeds: Pugs, Pekingese, Bichon Frises, Maltese

Aqua pops on a stunning white coat.

The Spring palette includes:

- ❋ Neutrals: ivory, light to medium beiges, light to medium browns, warm gray, and navy
- ❋ Violet, periwinkle, true blue, aqua, and turquoise
- ❋ Apricot, peach, salmon, corals warm pink, clear bright red, light orange, and orange-red
- ❋ Pastel to bright yellow green, golden yellow, and clear gold
- ❋ Jewelry: gold

Summer

Hair: ash blonde, light ash brown

Eyes: blue gray or blue green

Typical breeds: Chihuahuas, Shih Tzu, Chinese Crested Dogs

The Summer palette includes:

- ❋ Neutrals: soft white, rose-beiges, rose-browns, blue-gray, navy
- ❋ Powder blue from light to medium, periwinkle, aqua, blue-greens from light to deep

❋ Blue pinks from light to medium, watermelon red, blue-red, burgundy

❋ Lavender, raspberry, soft fuchsia, plum, and lemon yellow

❋ Jewelry: silver

Of course, it's a little harder with dogs than with humans! After all, how many humans come in spots? Still, it's fun to think about and to experiment with which colors look best on your dog.

Whether your dog is fabulous in fuchsia or best in burgundy, just have fun with it. We all know that what really counts most is that you adore your dog—whatever the season of his fur, or the season of his life; and you know that your dog feels the same way about you.

Is your Shih Tzu a Summer?

Chapter 2

Sweaters, Jackets, and Coats: Happiness Is a Warm Puppy

Charlie Brown had it right—happiness is a warm puppy. Even though Snoopy was comfortable sleeping in the snow on top of his dog house, your pooch would rather stay warm in a comfy sweater, jacket, or coat.

Sweaters

Today's dog sweaters are quality garments. Forget those silly little acrylic things pet stores carried once upon a time. Nowadays, sweaters come in fine wools, angora, mohair, and even cashmere. Styles range from the classic turtlenecks to fisherman's knits to off-the-shoulder elegance.

Finding the Right Fit

It can be tricky finding the perfect fit for a sweater. Doggie duds are usually sized by the length of the body, not the girth. Frankly, the system doesn't work well. It would be just as silly as going to the department store and finding clothes sized by height. We know that women can be 5 feet tall (1.5 m) and be a size 16, or be 6 feet tall (1.8 m) and be a size 10.

An 8-pound (3.6 kg) Papillon and an 18-pound (8.2 kg) Pug might both have a back that's 12 inches (30.5 cm) long. That 12-inch sweater is going to fit one of them a lot better than it fits the other one. Sweaters do have some leeway, since they stretch, but the only way to know for sure that something will fit is for your dog to try it on.

- Look for a comfortable fit around the neck. We all hate the feeling of a turtleneck sweater that's too tight, and your dog is no different!
- Check to see that the legs are a comfortable fit. If the sweater has sleeves, can the dog walk and move freely? Are the armholes large enough to allow movement, but snug enough to keep the warmth inside the sweater?
- Some sweaters are held on with various types of straps and ties. Make sure they're loose enough to be comfortable, and tight enough so that they won't get snagged when your dog plays in the sweater. Don't forget about the, uh, personal issues. Be sure there is plenty of clearance for pottying!
- If your long-haired dog has just been groomed (or is just about to be) remember that the amount of hair he's sporting at the moment affects the fit.

Getting In and Out

Be sure that it's easy for your dog to get in and out of the sweater. Some sweaters just seem to be a struggle to get on your little dog, while others are easy to get on and off. Have your dog try on the sweater, even if a friend swears the sweater works perfectly for her dog. (The same sweater may be

When fitting a sweater, remember to account for your dog's hair.

Trying It On for Size

All pet stores and pet boutiques will welcome a well-behaved dog on leash. You might be surprised that a lot of department stores will accept your dog as well. Upscale stores like Saks and Bergdorf Goodman will welcome your pooch with a smile.
Be sure to patronize those places where your dog is welcome. And when your dog isn't invited into a store? Let the retailer know that you're taking your business to the competition because they welcome dogs. When retailers learn that they do more business by welcoming dogs than by excluding them, you'll find a lot more stores will become pet-friendly!

easy to get on and off one dog, but difficult for another. For example, a sweater that's an easy fit for a sleek Miniature Pinscher might not work so well for a portly Pekingese.)

Cardigan sweaters (not to be confused with Cardigan Welsh Corgis, a lovely breed that definitely isn't a buttoned-down kind of dog) usually zip or button up. It's easiest if they close on the back, rather than the front of your pup.

Zippers can make it easier to get in the sweater, but be sure that zipper isn't going to get caught in your dog's coat, and that it's easy to slide together. Some sweaters come with Velcro fasteners. Again, if your dog has long hair, make sure that the Velcro is placed in a way that doesn't Velcro your dog to the sweater!

Two Legs or Four?

Some sweaters have sleeves for all four legs. These add extra warmth for your little guy, but take twice the fitting. Be double-sure you can put this sweater on and off easily before you buy it.

Look for Quality

Quality and a high price aren't necessarily the same. Make sure that seams are well-sewn, and the yarn is soft and comfortable. Most dogs have naked little tummies, and this material will be touching that tender spot, so make sure the sweater feels good to the touch. Plus, most likely you'll be holding your dog in your arms, so you'll want a sweater that makes him just as much fun to snuggle as he is when he's undressed.

All yarns are not created equal. Generally, natural yarns such as wool provide the most warmth, so look for those if you expect the sweater to keep him comfortable outside on a blustery day. If you live in a warmer climate, or if the sweater is mostly for indoor use, synthetic fabrics like acrylic are fine.

Remember Your Leash, Collar, or Harness

Your dog will he wearing his sweater outside, which means he'll also be on a leash. Check for both fashion and fit—make sure his collar looks good with the sweater, and that the neck of the sweater doesn't get in the way of the collar and leash.

Some sweaters come with a hole for the leash—the collar can be worn under the sweater, and the leash can comfortably snap on. Similarly, if your dog wears a harness, look for the new styles of sweaters that have holes for the leash to attach to the harness and allow your dog to wear his harness underneath the sweater.

Style, Style, Style!

Gone are the days when all dog sweaters looked the same. Today, a fantastic range of choices is available. A quick glance at Internet boutiques and stores showed sweaters adorned with hearts, crystals, fire hydrants, bows and bow ties, buttons, pockets, and sewn-on scarves. They came trimmed with lace, denim, feathers, fur, faux fur, leather, and wool fringe.

So, you can have just as much fun shopping for your little guy as you do for yourself!

Sweaters for People Who Don't Knit

You might be surprised to learn that you don't need to know a knitting needle from the Space Needle to make a cool sweater. Here's how:

"Sleeve Dogs"

In ancient China, little Pekingese and Shih Tzu were called "sleeve dogs,"

Feathers and Fur Trims

Dogs eat things that used to be alive. Think about that before you invest in a sweater with a feather boa or fur trim. Sooner or later, you'll carelessly leave a feather boa sweater on a chair, and your dog will think it's the best dog toy ever invented—and you plunked down quite a bit of money for this wonderful "toy." If you're too taken with feathers or fur to resist, just be sure you keep them away from your little guy when they are not being worn. For my own "fashionbeastas," I've decided the best choice is faux fur or fake feather fringes.

because the empress could carry these dogs in the sleeves of her clothing. You can use the sleeve of a human sweater to make your small dog a sweater of his own, so your dog will be something of a "sleeve dog," too.

It's easy. Start with a sweater you no longer wear—maybe that favorite cashmere sweater that got the unfortunate stain last time you wore it. Measure the length you want the dog sweater to be (adding a bit more for a hem) and cut. The ribbing at the sweater's wrist makes a perfect turtleneck for a little dog.

Cut holes for the legs. Hem around the armholes and hemline, and viola, you have a dog sweater. You can make one in minutes. Add trim to make it fashionable, like faux fur along the hem and arm holes. Add beads, buttons, and rhinestones—anything fun that reflects your dog's personality.

Look for sweaters that fit well, and are stylish.

Do you and your little dog share the same taste in clothes? Next time you find a sweater that's a real bargain, buy two. Make a "sleeve dog" sweater for your little pup, and you'll have matching outfits. Wear yours with pearls, and sew pearl beads onto your little dog's version.

Recycled Sweaters

You might have a favorite doggie sweater that perfectly fits your little guy, but it's old, or isn't made of great quality materials. You can use the old sweater as a pattern for a new one.

Cut the old dog sweater along its seam lines to make the pattern. Trace the shape onto a piece of paper. Then, find a human sweater (one of yours, one you find at a bargain price, or one you pick up at resale store) and cut the sweater along the pattern lines. Sew securely (do a whip-stitch around any exposed fabric edges to make sure it doesn't unravel). Trim it with ribbons, beads, buttons—whatever suits your fancy.

Now you have a new outfit for a fraction of the price of a purchased one, and you're doing your part to recycle. And dogs who recycle are always chic!

Sweaters for Crafty People

Knitting isn't just for grandma anymore—it's one of the biggest trends among hipsters. Go to urban hang-outs everywhere, and you'll see the sophisticated ladies (and a few men) purling away at "stitch and bitch" sessions. If you want to stitch for your bitch, companies that have traditionally given instruction on how to make human sweaters, hats, and afghans (the blankets, not the dogs) now have options for dogs.

Stores that carry good-quality yarn will offer a variety of dog sweater

DIY Tip

Wonderful sweaters are to be had at resale clothing stores—these are sweaters that are "last season," or out of repair, but still have sleeves in good shape. Some of these finds are made of fine wools, silk, or even cashmere. The sleeves from men's sweaters will fit slightly larger dogs, and the sleeves from children's sweaters will fit a tiny pup.

patterns. You can also check out the Internet, for places like Karp Styles (www.karpstyles.com), which has a book of patterns for dog sweaters or coats. Fiber Trends (www.fibertrends.com) has one pattern for a cute sweater (complete with fire hydrants) for a small dog, with matching socks for the human. Those of us with little dogs can have ankles that match our doggie designs!

Sweater or Coat?

When you go outside on a below-freezing day, you don't wear a light sweater—you wear a warm coat. Your dog should do the same. His sweater has limitations, just like yours. If you're looking for substantial warmth, get a coat.

You also can find several free patterns on the Internet. Just type in "dog sweater knitting instructions" in any search engine, and a number of choices will pop up. Most of these patterns work fine for an experienced knitter, but the instructions in the professionally packaged sweater patterns are clearer for the novice knitter. It's worth spending a few dollars for clear instructions if you're a beginner.

Happiness is indeed a warm puppy. With countless places to buy great sweaters, and several ways to make one yourself, you will have one chic and contented canine this winter!

A jacket must fit a dog comfortably around the neck and chest.

Jackets and Coats

Dogs come with their very own fur coats, provided by Mother Nature. So, it may seem silly to buy them a jacket for winter. The truth is that little dogs lose their body

Faux fur is always fabulous!

heat more quickly than the big bowsers. Small, slender, short-haired dogs, such as short-coated Chihuahuas, Miniature Pinschers, and Italian Greyhounds absolutely need help staying warm when they're outside on a cold day. Or, if you own a "naked," hairless breed like a Chinese Crested Dog, American Hairless Terrier, or Xoloitzcuintli (Mexican Hairless Dog), he's every bit as exposed to the dangers of the cold as a human baby.

For other breeds, coats are optional, depending on the circumstances. Moderately cold weather usually doesn't faze the longer-haired breeds, or even short-haired dogs with thick coats, such as Pugs. Some little guys even thrive on cold weather: Pomeranians are descendants of full-sized sled dogs, and most love a romp in the snow.

However, even the heartiest little dog needs help on some days. In bitterly cold weather, all dogs need protection, regardless of the length of their fur. Cold, penetrating rain also can be dangerous.

Whether you're getting a jacket for your dog for serious protection in a harsh climate, or just for a little fashion fun, be sure think through this purchase!

Warmth

If you live in the Midwest or Northeast, you purchase your own coats with care. You look for good construction, and wool or microfiber fabrics that retain warmth. Use the same good sense in selecting your dog's winter jackets.

If you live in a climate that experiences a cold winter, forget acrylic and look for materials such as wool and fleece. Feel the coat. Is it made of good construction? Does it cover the dog enough to envelop his body in warmth?

Fit

Like sweaters, a jacket must fit a dog comfortably around the neck and chest. The armholes should be comfortable. There should be clearance for potty functions. The difference between sweaters and jackets, of course, is that sweaters stretch. If you are investing in a serious winter jacket, take your dog with you when you buy it, so that he can try it on.

Cost

Designer dog coats can cost hundreds of dollars. Coats at large pet supply stores can retail for less than $20. While you don't need to spend a fortune on a coat, if you're looking for good-quality products to keep your little guy snug in a Minnesota or Maine winter, do expect to pay a little more. Of course, cost doesn't always equal quality, so look over the product carefully when you purchase it.

Lycra Body Suits

A great alternative to traditional coats are Lycra body suits for dogs, like those made by K9 Top Coat (www.k9topcoat.com). These suits look a little bit

Lycra body suits are a great idea for an active little dog.

weird at first—kind of like a scuba outfit for your dog. However, they are practical. The Lycra is stretchy, so the product fits well on most sizes and shapes of dogs. Their coats have legs built into them, so the whole dog is kept warm. Their Arctic Fleece Top Coat is lined with microfiber fleece, making it a warm, flexible product. The company also has a waterproof version of the coat for rainy climates. Their original Lycra suit provides basic protection against cool weather.

Your pup may get more stares than admiring glances with this product, but he'll love the warmth and comfort.

Raincoats

Don't snicker at the thought of a rain slicker—they can come in handy for your little dog. Short-coated little dogs can quickly become miserable in the rain. In addition, many of the small breeds have single, silky coats. So, instead of having a harsh outer coat that keeps off rain and snow and a cozy undercoat that provides insulation, breeds such as Yorkies, Papillons, Silky Terriers, and Japanese Chin just have a single layer of silken fur. That silky coat provides little protection from the rain.

If you live in the Pacific Northwest or another rainy climate, your little guy would probably appreciate some rain gear. That way you'll both be protected on your walks.

Hats and Hoods

Hats and hoods seem like such a great idea. For starters, they're adorable on a dog. Plus, we know that we humans lose most of our heat from our heads; we really can't be warm on a cold day without a nice wool hat or a hood on our coats.

Dogs see it differently. Even a Pekingese sees the world a little bit like a wolf does. In the wolf pack (and at the dog park) head postures tell a lot about who's in charge. Dominant dogs stand over a subordinate dog. The dominant dog will mouth the muzzle of his subject, letting him know in doggie language just who is in charge. Dogs use the position of their heads to tell each other where they belong in the pack.

Choose a jacket that fits your dog's personality.

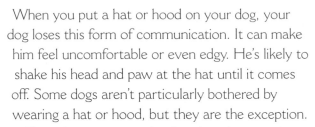

When you put a hat or hood on your dog, your dog loses this form of communication. It can make him feel uncomfortable or even edgy. He's likely to shake his head and paw at the hat until it comes off. Some dogs aren't particularly bothered by wearing a hat or hood, but they are the exception. If you buy a coat with a hood, make sure the hood hangs in a way that is comfortable for the dog if he doesn't want the hood on his head.

Fitting a Hat

If your dog doesn't mind having his head covered, and you'd like to buy him a hat, be sure to purchase one that attaches firmly in place. It should have a chin strap, and it must be comfortable for his ears. Small dogs have an infinite variety of ears shapes, from long-eared Beagles to Papillons, with ears that look like butterfly wings. Also, the size and shape of little-dog heads are hugely different, from the dome of a Chihuahua to the square head of a Pug. One size hat certainly does not fit all.

Whether your dog wears a designer wool coat, a Lycra body suit, or the fur coat Nature gave him, enjoy your dog during winter. Little dogs love walks at least as much as big ones do, and you'll have a great time strutting through the 'hood with tour little hound. Have fun year-round!

Chapter 3

Collars & Leashes:
Fit, Fashion, & Finding Your Way Home

A collar: It's your dog's most practical possession. It allows your little guy to go for a walk. It gives you something to hold on to when your dog would rather be chasing the cat. It hold the identification that can be his ticket home if he gets lost. But a collar is also your dog's most obvious fashion statement. It can show the world just how pampered and stylish your little dog is.

Of course, every dog needs at least one collar—but your dog might enjoy having several! After all, you really only need one pair of shoes, but chances are you have many pairs in your closet. It's both fun and practical to have the right shoes for every occasion, and the same goes for collars—there's nothing wrong with having just the right collar for every occasion.

Fabulous Collars Throughout History

Celebrities are often photographed with their petite pooches, who more often than not are wearing some fabulous-looking sparkly collar. From Audrey Hepburn and Elizabeth Taylor to Paris Hilton and Jennifer Lopez, the rich and famous love to splurge on fashionable collars for their dogs.

But these ladies weren't the first fashionistas to give their dogs fancy collars. Throughout history, people have adorned their dog's necks with everything from spikes to jewels.

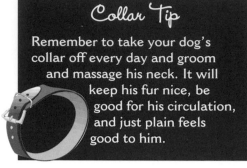

Collar Tip

Remember to take your dog's collar off every day and groom and massage his neck. It will keep his fur nice, be good for his circulation, and just plain feels good to him.

Back in the fifteenth, sixteenth, and seventeenth centuries, hunting dogs wore broad, iron collars bristling with fearsome-looking spikes to protect them from bears, wolves, and wild boar. Later, dog collars were used for decoration and identification, just as they are today. Fanciers in Germany, Austria, and England adorned their dogs with beautiful brass collars, sometimes decorated with velvet.

There's even a dog-collar museum at Leeds Castle in England, where a half million tourists have seen a collection of collars from medieval times to the nineteenth century. Some of those ancient collars include the same kind of information we put on modern-day dog tags. One fanciful eighteenth century English brass collar in the collection reads: I am Mr Pratt's Dog, King St, Nr Wokingham, Berks. Whose Dog are You?

Throughout history, people have adorned their dog's necks with fancy collars.

We aren't the first generation to love our dogs, and want them to be just as fashionable—and just as happy—as we are.

The Basics: Fit

Finding a collar that fits a little dog can be harder than finding one for a full-sized dog. However, it's important that you make the effort for your dog's comfort and safety. Here's why:

❈ An ill-fitting collar can create sores.

❈ A collar that's too loose will allow your dog to slip out.

❈ A collar that's too flimsy can break just when you need it most.

Not Too Big

A little dog with a huge collar and leash always looks so sad—it reminds me of the little dog in *How the Grinch Stole Christmas*, pathetically pulling the heavy sled with his oversized collar.

But a big collar isn't just silly-looking—it can chafe and irritate your dog's throat.

Happily, most large pet supply stores and many pet boutiques now carry the right-sized collars for smaller dogs. Little guys under about 8 pounds (3.6 kg) or so should have a collar that's 3/8-inch (.95 cm) wide. Slightly bigger dogs may need a 5/8-inch (1.6 cm) collar.

How to Find Products for Tiny Little Dogs

It's a lot easier than it used to be to find little collars and leashes. Most large pet supply stores carry right-sized products, and so do many specialty boutiques. Plenty of Internet sites also offer products for tiny dogs, if you can't find a product that fits your dog at your local store. Almost all dog shows have vendors selling products for pint-sized pooches, and it's a lot of fun to go to a show not only to shop, but to look at the incredible variety of dogs. (You can find a list of upcoming shows at www.akc.org.)

Not Too Small

If you have a bigger, more active dog, be sure that the collar is sturdy enough. An active terrier who flies to the end of his leash at the sight of a cat should be fitted with a slightly larger collar rather than a smaller one. You don't want the collar to break the moment you need it. For sturdier dogs, make sure the materials are sturdy. Look for well-constructed buckles and collars made of leather or other materials that won't fall apart when a determined little dog throws all his g-forces against the leash.

Not Too Loose

It's important for your dog's collar to be secure around his neck. Otherwise, he'll quickly learn to duck his head out of the collar, and then you're stuck holding the leash while your dog runs through the neighborhood.

A general "rule of thumb" is to use your thumb (or other fingers). Put your finger inside the collar. If you can fit more than one finger comfortably between the collar and your dog's neck, the collar on a small dog is too loose.

Also, look at the size of your dog's head! If he's got a big neck and a little head, the collar has to be fitted fairly snugly around his neck. If he's got a skinny neck and a larger head, the collar can be looser, without worrying about your dog slipping out of it.

Not Too Tight

A surprising number of otherwise really smart people get a collar for their puppies and never think to check how tight it grows over time. Check regularly to see if your dog's collar is comfortable. Even when he stops growing taller, a dog may fill out with muscle until he's about 3 or 4 years old. Also, if he's a long-haired dog, he'll probably have more fur in winter, so the collar needs to be loosened in winter and tightened again in summer after he sheds his winter fur.

Not Too Feline

People with little dogs are often tempted to buy their dog a cat collar—after all, they fit. Don't do it! Cat collars have break-away features that allow the cat to escape if the collar becomes entangled on a branch, fence, or other obstacle. That break-away feature has saved a lot of cats' lives.

However, the last thing in the world that you want is your dog's collar to fall apart just as you're grabbing it. The whole point of a dog collar is to have something that doesn't break away when you need it. Leave the cat collars to the cats.

Just Right

Put some thought into your dog's collar. He wears it 24 hours a day, 7 days a week. Be sure it's comfortable and fits well. Check that it doesn't chafe against his skin. It matters that your little dog is not only stylish, but comfortable.

A Word of Caution

Collars and ID tags save lives, but they can also cost your dog his life if you aren't careful. If your dog is confined at home in a wire crate or exercise pen, it's possible for him to catch his collar or tags on the wire, with disastrous results. Especially if you have a frisky puppy (or frisky adult dog), take the collar off before confining him in a location where he could catch his collar on something. An alternative is to use a cat-style break-away collar just for when he's confined, then replace it with a collar that won't come apart when he's out and about.

Collar Materials: Think Quality and Comfort

Whether you're paying $6, $60, or $600 for a collar, think about quality and comfort before you buy. Here are some things to consider before choosing a collar.

Leather

Leather collars range from comfy to miserable. Feel the leather before you buy. Does it feel buttery and smooth? Are there uncomfortable seams that will dig into your little dog's neck? Rolled collars, in which the leather is rolled into a round shape, are generally easier on coats than flat collars.

Leather collars can get softer with time. Before putting the collar on your dog's neck, spend an hour or so rubbing and stretching the collar to make it as soft as possible. (You can do this while you're relaxing and watching Animal Planet re-runs with your little guy.)

Look for colors and patterns that are pleasing to your eye. You can go girly and pink, or find a gorgeous Western design. Spend a little extra if you can, since a leather collar is a life-time investment.

Fabric

Little dogs don't need the strength of a leather collar to keep them under control. Fabric collars are lightweight and are usually more comfortable than any but the best leather collars. They're also inexpensive, so you can buy a wonderful variety of colors and patterns. Fabric collars aren't "investment dressing," but they are practical and fun. Because fabric collars are less expensive, be extra careful about checking the buckle or snap. Be sure it's strong enough for your dog, that it closes securely, and that it unsnaps easily. Safety still counts!

Fabulous Fashions!

There's a wonderful, endless variety of beautiful collars to choose from. You can shop online, at large pet supply stores, and at trendy boutiques. It's a lot of fun to take your dog window shopping with you. Go ahead and try on some collars and see what suits him best. Laugh with each other at the goofy stuff, drool together at the beautiful items, and enjoy the time together.

Want a collar with a skull and crossbones? Who doesn't? Or a pink collar with rhinestones when your girl needs to look like a princess? Some collars and leashes are made from the incredibly soft leather of a kangaroo. Other collars are bejeweled with real diamonds—or with gems that are patently fun fakes. From serious to silly, there are collars for every dog and every day.

Spending the Big Bucks

Planning to splurge four digits on a real diamond collar? Purchase your major expenditure with all the same care you'd spend on a jewelry purchase for yourself. Look for quality of construction, quality of the stones, and aesthetics. Do it right, and your dog's collar might land in a dog-collar museum some day. Do it wrong, and you'll just feel foolish.

Purple on your Rat Terrier is always in fashion.

Diamonds Are a Dog's Best Friend!

They say dog is man's best friend, and diamonds are a girl's best friend, so it seems only natural when men and women give diamonds to their dogs. Where to find sparkle for your Shih Tzu? Kings Jewelers has an upscale line called Fancy Bones. They have an 8-inch (20 cm) diamond collar with nearly 6 carats of diamonds which will set you back $7,500. They also have charms and ID tags made of gold and precious jewels. For example, their diamond ID bone sparkles with 3.40 carats of gem diamonds. The back is flat, with room for engraving your dog's return information—all for a mere $4,500.

And, since you'll want to look just as good as your dog, Fancy Bones has dog jewelry for humans. You can purchase a human version of the dog-bone ID tag, made of 18 karat gold with 4.11 carats of diamonds, for $5,500.

The company promises to give a little bit of love with every purchase, donating a portion of the proceeds from the Fancy Bone jewelry to the Humane Society of Greater Miami. Check them out at www.fancybones.com.

Do It Yourself!

Even if you aren't a Martha Stewart, you can make fancy, fun dog collars for any occasion. All it takes is a quick trip to a craft store and an inexpensive fabric collar.

Craft stores are full of all the same beads, baubles, and buttons that you see on expensive dog collars—and those beads can cost as little as a dollar or two for a dozen or more. All you have to do is sew or glue the beads or buttons on to a plain fabric collar, and you have a fun, fashionable, flashy collar with an inexpensive price tag.

Beads, Rhinestones, Paws, and Happy Faces!

If you haven't been to a craft store in recent years, you'll be amazed at the choices of beads and buttons available. A recent trip to a popular craft chain store provided buttons in the shapes of bones and paws, not to mention fire hydrants and cats. Use your imagination to create the perfect collar for your dog's personality.

I found shiny beads in butterfly shapes perfect for my Papillons, and gold-colored butterfly charms were less than a dollar apiece.

 Does your little dog volunteer as a therapy dog, visiting people in nursing homes, schools, or hospitals? You might want to sew happy face buttons to his collar. You can even sew some on your own T-shirt, and the two of you will match!

 You can find holiday bracelet kits that include enough beads to decorate a small red collar. There was also a Hanukkah bracelet, with silver and blue beads that would look pretty on a blue collar.

All these collar projects can be done with a needle and thread; or you can spring for that glue gun if you're aiming to be Martha's next apprentice.

Necklaces, Neckties, and Bowties

Do you have a special occasion coming up? Of course you do, since every day with your dog is special. It can be fun to give your dog a necklace, necktie, or bowtie to wear on that special day.

You can purchase specially sized neckties for little dogs. There's just something so sweet and serious about a furry little guy in a tie. (And men can buy human neckties with dogs on them—sort of a matching outfit.) And with necklaces the big fashion item of the year for women, it's no surprise that beaded dog necklaces are also popular.

Remember, these fun items don't take the place of a sturdy collar. Necklaces can break, and can also dig into your little doggie diva's skin if you aren't careful.

Ah, the timelessness of pearls.

"Collar ID"

Every dog should have an identification tag on at all times. Dogs escape, and the best way to ensure a happy reunion is to keep your dog identified at all times. Now, you may be telling yourself that you aren't the kind of person whose dog wanders off, and you certainly don't have a little hobo dog who wants to roam away from home. Your dog would rather be under your feet than running down the road.

Even the best owners and best dogs can get separated. Older dogs often start roaming, probably for much the same reason that older people with Alzheimer's disease feel the need to wander. Even good dogs will check out what's on the other side of the fence if a meter reader accidentally left a gate open. And what if you're in a car accident? The separation of people and pets in the aftermath of recent natural disasters is also a reminder that every dog needs a tag.

However, most small-dog owners don't keep identification on their dogs' collars. Why? Those big, clunky tags can snarl and damage long hair. Plus, it's a large piece of hardware on a tiny dog, which can be uncomfortable when he's trying to lie down and relax. Not to mention a little dog with a big tags sort of looks like a dude from the 1970s, with a large medallion hanging down his chest (and people snickered at those guys even back then).

Happily, some alternatives work better for little dogs than a stark metal tag.

> ## What Not to Wear
>
> Don't buy a choke collar for your little dog! Little dogs have slender throats, and a choke collar can cause serious damage. Many small-breed dogs have problems with collapsing tracheas—windpipes that are weak and easily damaged. A choke collar makes this very serious health problem worse. C'mon, it's not like you can't control little Fluffy without a choke collar. Don't buy one.

Sliders

Sliders are just what they sound like—tags that slide onto the collar rather than hang from it. They're much easier on your dog's coat, and much less bulky for a little dog. One company you might want to check out is Boomerang Tags (www.boomerangtags.com).

Pouches

Many pet supply stores sell fabric pouches that cover metal tags. This provides a little more comfort for your small dog, and eliminates the constant jangling sound of tags.

Collars With ID

It may not be particularly fashionable, but it is extremely practical to buy a collar with your dog's name and your phone number stitched right into the collar. Then, you don't have to worry about tags at all (and hey, you might even start a new fashion trend!). A few sources of this sort of collar exist; one is Dog.com (www.dog.com), which has affordable collars available in small sizes.

Like the idea of a phone number on the collar, but still want some bling? In the Company of Dogs (www.inthecompanyofdogs.com) has personalized rhinestone collars for sale. Instead of ordering your pet's name on the collar, order your phone number.

Custom-Made Tags

Want something beautiful and different? Talk with your local jeweler. There's no reason that your tag can't be a delicate work of engraved gold.

However you do it, just do it. Be sure your dog is identifiable, so that he can get home to you.

Collar Do's

Whether you're spending a few dollars on a practical collar or a few thousand to show the world that you think of your pooch as top dog, you should enjoy finding a collar that's just right for him. Just like dogs since medieval times, your dog's collar not only says something about him, but about your relationship with him.

Keep tabs on your dog with ID tags.

Tech Talk—The Next Big Thing

What's the next big thing in keeping tabs on your pet? Global positioning systems. The same technology that allows On-Star to call for help if your car is stolen (or you get lost) is available for your pet. In 2005, the Globalpetfinder came on the market, a device that straps onto a dog's collar or harness and then sends location alerts to your cell phone, pager, or computer. The Globalpetfinder is pricey, and the technology isn't practical yet for small-sized dogs (the device weighs 5 ounces (.14 kg) and is bulky), but as the device gets smaller, and the price comes down, look for this technology to become a lot more common.

Until global positioning systems are practical for our pint-sized pooches, keep the collar and tags on your dog—they're his best chance to finding his way home.

Microchipping: High Tech for Little Dogs

The easiest way to get your lost dog returned is a tag with your phone number on it. Still, there are times when a collar slips off a lost dog. He also might zip through the door in that one moment he isn't wearing his collar. Your dog needs a back-up security system. Happily, using today's technology, the answer is easy and inexpensive.

Microchips are rice-sized computer chips with a unique number. Your veterinarian will insert the chip under your dog's skin—a process no more painful than getting a vaccine. If your dog is lost, most veterinary clinics and animal shelters have scanners that read these chips. They make a quick call to the microchip company, and you get a call saying your pet is safe and sound and wants to come home!

Do they work? You bet. There are countless tales of animals reunited with their owners because of a microchip scan at a shelter. When Hurricane Katrina (2005) separated thousands of people and their pets, many dogs were reunited with their owners because the animals had a microchip.

Finding a Leash: The Basics

Finding a great leash is like finding the perfect pair of comfortable shoes. You spend countless hours with your dog on that leash, and it's worth investing in

Don't let your little dog get away! Keep ID tags on him when you go out.

something that's comfortable for you to hold in your hand, lightweight for your dog, and that looks good. And hey, it's a bonus if your favorite leash happens to match your favorite pair of shoes!

Your little dog's leash should be lightweight and comfortable. A big, heavy leash isn't any fun for your dog, and can leave him looking like he's a prisoner on a chain gang. For small dogs, leashes should be 3/8-inch (1.2 cm) wide.

The best length of lead is either 4 or 6 feet (1.2 or 1.8 m); both lengths keep your dog near you, but give enough leeway for some sniffing along the way. I personally prefer a 6-foot (1.8 m) lead, to give the dog a little extra freedom.

Whether you purchase a leather or fabric leash, you should look for one that folds comfortably into your hand. You should be able to reel it in and out with your fingers. One of the advantages of having a small dog is that a small leash is much less cumbersome than a big dog's heavy leash!

Quality

When looking for a leash, quality counts. Remember, you and your dog are attached by the leash for hours a day, as you walk, shop, and run errands together. Leashes really are a place for "investment dressing" your dog! Consider the following before you buy:

- ❀ If you're looking for a leather leash, close your eyes and feel the leather. Is it soft and pliable? Does it feel good—even sensuous—in your hand?
- ❀ Do the same with fabric leashes. Can you crumple the fabric up and release it comfortably?
- ❀ Look carefully at the hardware. Does the snap open easily (you don't want to struggle to get the leash on and off) and shut securely (you don't want the dog's collar jiggling out of the leash)?
- ❀ Check out the leash construction. Is the stitching on the leash where the snap connects and the handle is formed strong and secure?
- ❀ Sometimes, inexpensive fabric leashes are glued rather than stitched. Before you consider buying a glued leash, even for a one-time use, pull at the glued area. Is it firmly in place, or can you feel the fabric come apart? Don't ever put your dog on a leash that can come unglued!

In short: whatever size, price range, shape, and color you prefer, remember that safety comes first. After all, the reason we have our little dogs on leashes in the first place is to keep them safe.

What Not to Wear

Here are some "don'ts" for your little dog.

Metal Chain Leashes

Metal chain leashes are impossibly heavy for your little dog, and may even be too much for larger dogs. If your dog pulls hard, they can hurt your hands as the chain slips across your skin. Worse yet, if you drop the leash, the metal can scare a running dog (making him run farther away), and could even injure him.

In short: Don't buy one.

Retractable Leashes

Retractable leashes are wildly popular, but I don't loke them for your little dog. They allow your dog to reel out a line that is as long as 25 feet (7.6 m).

Think about the length of that line when you're walking on city streets. If your little dog sees a kitty or squirrel, you don't have control for that 25 feet (7.6 m). If a car is coming, your dog can run right in front of it.

It's better to buy a 6-foot (1.8 m) leash and let your dog move around in that area. If you feel you absolutely must be a retractable lead, please, please, please be sure to keep the length of the leash locked into a distance that keeps your dog safe from traffic!

Lovely Leashes

Your dog's leash is often your best chance to show his style. If you have a long-haired dog, no one will even see his collar, so his leash is an even more important fashion statement.

You can find matching collars, leashes, and hair accessories for your pooch.

Color!

Who says that leather leashes have to be boring old brown things? Color is hip! Whether you're looking at your local boutique or getting your retail therapy on the Internet, leashes now come in a rainbow of colors. Your dog might look pretty in pink, but don't forget to look for luscious lavenders, burgundies, yellows, and blues.

Gems and Jewels

Little dogs were made for glam. Pet boutiques have a wonderful assortment of crystals, rhinestones, sequins, and other shiny pseudo-gems on leashes. It's fun to deck your dog in diamonds (real or faux).

Do be sure that the bling doesn't get in the way of the comfort and utility of the leash. Pick it up, hold it, pretend you're walking your dog. (Okay, people might look at you funny, but still put your hands on the leash.) You don't want rhinestones cutting into the palms of your hands, so be sure that the leash is comfortable for a walk, as well as totally adorable for your dog.

Exotic Leathers

Leashes are available in all the great leathers, from fine latigo leather to even kangaroo and ostrich. How about going line dancing in your ostrich cowgirl boots, accompanied by your dog in an ostrich leash?

Check Your Hardware Regularly!

The snaps on leashes grow old. Buckles on collars can get worn. Old hardware isn't as sturdy as new. Keep your dog safe by making sure his leashes and collars are in good condition.

Build Your Own Leash!

Just as you can make a flashy collar from inexpensive materials, you can do the same for leashes. Here are a few ideas.

Decorate a Matching Collar and Leash

Inexpensive collars usually have matching inexpensive fabric leashes. Sew on matching beads and buttons, either along the entire leash or just at the stitching where the snap is held and the leash handle is formed.

Look for Sturdy Materials

Be sure the ribbon or cord you select is sturdy enough for your dog. For example, craft and fabric stores often have pretty, narrow strips of leather—about the width you'd use for a shoe lace. Even a 5-pound (2.3 kg) dog can snap those delicate leather strings, so avoid them. Some ribbon is very strong, but others will easily pull apart with any pressure. You don't want to use elastic—it will turn your dog leash into a bungee cord!

Make a Leash from Velvet, Gold Cord, and Other Cool Stuff

If you've never spent time at craft or sewing stores, you'll be amazed at the fun things there are to buy. You can buy long strips of velvet, wonderful varieties of gold cords, and a host of other ribbons and cords.

Remember to buy enough extra inches to fold the fabric over to sew in the leash snap and to make the loop for a handle. Buy about an extra foot of material; purchase 7 feet (2.1 m) of cord rather than 6 feet (1.8 m) to make a 6-foot (1.8 m) leash.

You can find dog leash snaps at many craft stores (they're used in making purses and key chains). You can also use a snap from one of your old leashes, as long as the snap is still in good condition.

When comparing the prices between buying a fashion leash and making your own, you'll be stunned at the difference. It's not unusual for the supplies to make and decorate for a 6-foot (1.8 m) leash to cost less than a few dollars.

Even those of us who aren't domestic divas can do this level of sewing! Just fold the cord over around the hook and sew. Do the same for the loop of the handle. You definitely don't need a sewing machine for this—you can sew by hand. Just be sure to do plenty of stitches and to overlap them, so that the leash is secure.

I've made velvet ribbon leashes for my dogs for years. Each dog has his or her own color, and we get lots of compliments. The velvet is strong and durable. I've had leather leashes break, but never a velvet one! When it's old, or you're tired of the color, you just toss the old leash and make a new one in a matter of minutes.

Harnesses: Not Just for Pulling Sleds

Some little dogs like to pull at the end of the leash, which can cause hacking and choking as the collar pulls against his neck. In this case, you might want to use a harness instead of a leash. It will put less pressure on his neck and throat, and you'll both be happier.

Harnesses have a second benefit for our little dogs: they are a great means to hoist your dog to safety. If you see a big dog coming toward your little dog, chances are you'll want to scoop up your dog in your arms.

The best harness for safely hoisting your little pooch comes from Ruff Wear, and was originally designed for search-and-rescue dogs and avalanche dogs. The harness was designed to allow handlers to lift their dogs from perilous places. The company makes the harness in a size to fit even tiny dogs, so your dog can be safely picked up from the perils of the sidewalk. You can check out the Web Master harness at www.ruffwear.com.

Of course, you can find harnesses with rhinestones and a little style, too. Your dog doesn't always have to look like he's going out on a search-and-rescue mission! As with collars, the most important thing is to check your harness for comfort and fit, and be sure to take the harness off your pup every day to comb and massage him.

Paws for a Good Cause

Several million people bought yellow plastic wrist bands to support bicyclist Lance Armstrong's fight to eradicate cancer. When we wear these wristbands, we're truly wearing our hearts on our sleeves. Your dog can show his support for a good cause, too. Remember, supporting a worthy cause is always in style!

- **Rally to Rescue:** Purina sells Rally to Rescue collars for dogs and matching wristbands for humans—all the money raised goes to nonprofit groups that help out homeless pets. Learn more about it at www.purina.com, or purchase one from a local nonprofit group participating in the program.
- **The Susan G. Komen Breast Cancer Foundation:** You might be one of the million people who run or walk in the Susan G. Komen Breast Cancer Foundation's Race for the Cure events held all around the country. Their symbol of hope is a pink ribbon. Some manufacturers sell leashes and collars with pink ribbons, with a portion of their profits going to the foundation. (You also might

think about making your own leash, or just tying a pretty pink ribbon around your dog's regular leash, and donate the whole cost of a new leash to the foundation.)

❀ **Support Your Local Animal Charities!** Chances are your local shelter has an annual walk or race to support their operations. Snap on your favorite fancy leash, lace up your sneakers, and have a great day with your dog. What better way to show off your dog's stylish leash than by helping out the dogs who aren't so lucky as yours.

Whether you buy a collar or leash that supports good cause, or make one of your own, I can't imagine a better day than one spent with friends and your dog, supporting a good cause.

Choose your materials carefully for DIY projects—your dog may find feathers irresistible.

Chapter 4

Fashion Hounds: Designers and Trends

Fashionable women love designers. There was a time when top designers had a famous, elegant woman attached to their designs. Oleg Cassini had Jackie O. and Givenchy had Audrey Hepburn—they created fashion icons still recognizable today. Designer clothes are still in fashion, with one tiny difference—designer labels are now available for your little dog.

Designer Duds

If you think it's only hype, take a look at some of the names that you can find on fashions for your dog:

- ❀ Gucci is one of the most recognizable logos in fashion today. The brand is carried at stores including Neiman Marcus and Saks. It's dog products includes rain coats ($165 in the small sizes), leash and collar sets ($425), small-dog carriers ($650), and vanilla-scented rubber bones ($65).
- ❀ Ralph Lauren has cashmere sweaters for dogs ($95). His polo shirts for your pooch ($32) bear the Ralph Lauren polo pony logo.

- ❀ The trendy Juicy Couture, a favorite of JLo, has pet carriers ($295) and pet carrier charms for your necklace ($50).
- ❀ The always-stylish Brit-brand Burberry, found at Nordstrom stores, features a shearling suede dog coat with hood and side pocket ($395).
- ❀ Shoe and handbag designer Donald J. Pliner created the Friends of Baby Doll Pliner line in honor of his Maltese. It features fashions for dogs weighing under 20 pounds (9 kg), including Italian leather carriers, dog collars, and leashes. His coats ($210 to $420) include a buckskin coat lined in butter-soft cashmere, hooded shearlings, and a day-glo coat trimmed in leather and lined with cashmere.
- ❀ Coach doesn't just make leather handbags anymore—they also make elegant collars and leashes for your little diva.
- ❀ Penhaligon's makes leashes ($125) and bone-design feeding bowls ($95).
- ❀ The biggest name (or at least the biggest price tag) is Louis Vuitton, whose carrier will set you back $1,470.

Yes, serious canine couture is here to stay.

And big retailers are recognizing this trend. Saks has an extensive pet department, and they welcome dogs in the Fifth Avenue store in New York. Nordstrom and Neiman Marcus carry designer dog items. Target knows how much the four-footed family members mean to their customers—they have a large selection of cool fashions in their pet department, including items from designer Isaac Mizrahi.

Celebrity Couture

Celebrities have gotten into canine fashion scene, too. Fashionista Paris Hilton has designed a line for "fashionbeastas," inspired by her Chihuahua, Tinkerbell. "In addition to my own sense of style, I think a lot of people admire Tinkerbell's look as well," she says. She's designed a dog necklace that's a simple chain with a bone outlined in crystals.

Pamela Anderson Pets, designed by none other than Baywatch babe Pamela Anderson, has a line of pet products featuring cute prints for your tiny sidewalk runway model. Playboy has graduated from bunny ears for playmates to leashes and collars with the bunny logo for your boy.

Pet fashions are a place for new and creative companies to take hold. Check out Little Lily, which designs exclusively for dogs, and you'll be impressed by their fashion sense. Ironically, Little Lily features a line of Hello Kitty dog clothes, so some of the trendiest dogs might end up wearing this hot cat logo.

Canine Couture: The Next Big Thing

Have you wondered what the well-dressed dog will be wearing over the next couple of years? Here's the predictions from some of the savviest people in the industry:

- **Pretty and Pink.** Everything pink and girly-girl is still hot, hot, hot. It's pink T-shirts, collars, coats, dog beds, and dresses. As the pink fad begins to wane, look for green to take its place—green may be the new pink.

- **The Metrosexual Male.** In urban areas, the metrosexual male is the man of the moment. They're the men who have great apartments, know what clothes are completely hip, and know the best places to dine. The metrosexual male has a metrosexual dog—maybe a Jack Russell Terrier or a French Bulldog. Expect that dog to wear cool designer wear, like a Ralph Lauren cashmere sweater. His accessories include the best leather collars, a portable water dish that folds into a pocket (so he's comfortable on his long walks), and a copy of the ultra-hip Bark magazine (for West Coast metrosexuals) and New York Dog magazine (for when he's on Eastern Time).

- **The Casual Male.** For the more casual guy, look for rugby shirts and Hawaiian prints.

- **Dresses.** Flirty girls love dresses. Look for feminine pink prom dresses and the little black dress, a classic that's always in style.

- **Boots.** Dogs are wearing footwear, er, pawwear. They range from Little Lily boots (that look like go-go boots, fur boots, and tennis shoes) to serious dog booties to protect against the elements.

Your fashion hound will look great in shades.

- **Leather.** Forget the tacky plastic coats that were supposed to look like motorcycle jackets. Now the real thing is available for your little dog. Quality leather goods are the rage, from jackets to fine collars and leashes. Look for exotic leathers such as snakeskin and ostrich.
- **Mother-Daughter Outfits.** Remember the moms who sewed those matching outfits for themselves and their daughters? They're baaaaaaack. Except now, they make matching sweaters for dog "moms" and their pooches. Don't want it too "matchy-matchy?" How about the human wearing a hat and scarf of the same yarn that's in the dog's sweater?
- **Jewelry.** In human fashion, necklaces and earrings are everywhere, and jewelry for your dog is just as hot. Whether it's hearts, stars, or 14-karat gold dog tags hanging from collars, or separate little dog necklaces, jewelry is hip. Consider a locket of your own with a photo of your dog.

T-Shirts: Making a Statement

Sweaters, jackets, collars, and leashes all have both form and function—they can be beautiful, but essentially they have serious uses. On the other hand T-shirts, which are a big trend in doggie wear, are just for fun. They're part of the glorious American tradition of expressing yourself. And now, you can express yourself (and the opinions of your little diva too, of course) with a cool slogan or fun graphic doggie tee.

"I borrowed this from Paris Hilton's dog."

There are dog T-shirts for every political bent, personal philosophy, and lifestyle. Your pooch doesn't mind being your spokesdog. After all, he thinks everything you say is wise, so he doesn't mind wearing your opinions on his sleeve (er, back). And he'll just love all the attention.

Political Doggedness

Let your pooch proudly display where your political heart lies. In the last presidential election, you could buy T-shirts that proclaimed which candidate your dog supported (even if he couldn't vote!). Then there were the post-election doggie T-shirts that said, "Don't blame me. I just voted for dinner."

Politically Incorrect

In the dog world, "Bitch" isn't a naughty word. So, of course, there are countless T-shirts making jokes about bitches. A few include:

- ❀ Alpha Bitch (written in rhinestones)
- ❀ Beautiful Bitch
- ❀ That's Ms. Bitch To You
- ❀ Bitches ♥ Me
- ❀ I hate Tinkerbell. That bitch has everything!

A Short List of T-Shirt Slogans

Say It To The Paw
I Need A Hug
Rock Star
Stud Muffin
Pamper Me Please
Wild Child
Diva (written in rhinestones)
Mine! Mine! Mine!
Flirty
Mommy's Little Girl
High Maintenance
Angel Face
Velcro
Zoom!
Toy Killer
Gas Powered
Earth Angel
Bite Me
What Would Scooby Do?
Am I Cute Or What?!
Girl's Rule!
Attitude Is Everything
Small But Lethal
Teacher's Pet (for a teacher)
My Owner's A Nerd (for computer geeks)

Better Than a Personal Ad

Some T-shirts help their owners find two-legged love (since you already have four-legged love). For example, one T-shirt says: Ask Me About My Owner:

Imitation: The Sincerest Form of Lawsuit

Some designers don't want to be associated with the doggie set. Just ask Tommy Hilfiger and his alter ego, Timmy Holedigger. Timmy Holedigger is a perfume for pets. Hilfiger's company sued the manufacturer, arguing that consumers might get the dog perfume confused with Hilfiger's designer line.

Ruling that the pet perfume company was within its rights to parody Hilfiger, Southern District of New York Chief Judge Michael B. Mukasey called Hilfiger's position "dour" and said the company "is 'advised to chill,'" according to an article by Tom Perrotta in the *New York Law Journal*. The opinion noted that "Hilfiger fails to see the humor in all this."

Nature Labs LLC, which makes Holedigger, also sells other parody fragrances for pets, including Bono Sports (Ralph Lauren's Polo Sports) and Miss Claybone (Liz Claiborne). The perfumes are have slogans like: "Strong enough for a man, but made for a Chihuahua."

In other cases, dog snacks named Fido-Lay and Dogiva were found to infringe the Frito-Lay and Godiva trademarks. The judge said that those cases didn't apply to the Hilfiger ruling, in part because pet perfume is inherently a parody item, whereas dog treats are not. Who knew?

What will the legal beagles, er, eagles come up with next?

Single, Nice Looking, Kind to Animals…AVAILABLE.

There is nothing your little dog can't do for you!

Make Your Own Statement

You might be inspired to make your own statement on a doggie-tee. Go to any office supply store, look in the label section, and you'll find prepackaged materials to make your own T-shirt transfers from your computer.

How about making a transfer of a photo of your dog, putting it on your T-shirt, and putting a photo of you on his? Do you support a good cause? Let your dog advertise it for you on his tee. How about promoting your business? A company in England hires large dogs and their owners to walk around wearing T-shirts that advertise various businesses. You small dog can be your mini-billboard.

Or Make No Statement

Sometimes plain, colorful T-shirts are enough for your little guy. Buy a T-shirt trimmed with lace, or one in hippie tie-dyed colors. Just a pretty pink tee says a lot, too. The bottom line is be creative and have fun.

The Future's So Bright, I Gotta Wear Shades

Sunglasses for your dog? You bet! Sunglasses and visors are a big trend for little dogs. There is something hilarious and fun about seeing a little dog in sunglasses. Believe it or not, there's a serious side to glasses and visors for your dog. For some dogs, glasses and visors can save their eyesight.

The Smush-Faced Breeds

You gotta love the sweet look of the flat-faced breeds, like Boston Terriers, Pugs, Pekingese, French Bulldogs, Japanese Chin, Brussels Griffons, Shih Tzu, and Affenpinschers. But that sweet, darling look comes with a price. In very flat-faced dogs, their eyes can actually protrude further than their noses, and that makes those eyes likely to hit things and cause injury.

There's another problem that can occur with dogs who are only somewhat short-faced: a change in how the nerves to the eyes work. Because of the change in structure, many dogs with flat faces feel little or no pain in their eyes. That may seem like a good thing, until your realize that your smush-faced dog isn't pulling away from danger because it doesn't hurt him. He can also have a serious eye injury that needs immediate attention, and you won't know it because he shows no signs of pain.

Protecting flat-faced dogs' eyes is important. It's a good idea for these dogs to have protection for their eyes, especially if they will be playing in grassy or woodsy areas.

Fun Tees!

The Internet is booming with fun, campy clothes for your little dog. One place to check out the most fashion-forward tees is www.Ruffruffandmeow.com.

Wind and Debris

Wind and debris is a problem for all eyes (including our own). If you drive a convertible, you probably wear sunglasses in part to keep the grit out of your eyes. If your little dog is a passenger, it's a good idea for him to wear glasses to protect his eyes, too.

If you regularly go to windy, gritty places, whether it's a house on the beach or a summer spot in the desert, protect your dog's eyes from grit and debris just as you do your own.

Glasses

By far, the biggest manufacturer of protective eyewear is Doggles, who produces very cool-looking goggle-style glasses for dogs. They look sort of like the glasses basketball stars wear.

Doggles come in clear and tinted shades, and several fashion colors. They come in a wide variety of sizes, fitting most dogs 5 pounds (2.2 kg) and larger. They are widely available at pet supply stores and boutiques. Check them out at www.doggles.com.

Visors and Hats

Glasses don't fit on all dogs. It's especially frustrating that flat-faced breeds, who most need eye protection, sometimes just can't make glasses fit on their little faces. For those dogs, consider a sun visor or hat with a brim that points out further than their vulnerable eyes.

Fit is everything in a hat or visor, so take your dog with you when you select a visor. Take your time to find one that works best with the size and shape of your dog's face

A visor can help protect vulnerable eyes.

and ears. This probably isn't a good Internet purchase until you find a brand that fits your dog, since dog head shapes vary so widely.

Teaching Your Dog to Enjoy Hats and Glasses

- ❀ **Make it fun.** Help your dog associate these weird items on his face and head with something pleasant. To a dog, pleasant means food! Show him the glasses, give him a treat. Hold the glasses near his face, give him a treat. Let him learn that this is a good thing—not an object of torture!
- ❀ **Give it a name.** When you put the glasses (or hat on), give it a word so that your dog knows what's coming. So, say "Glasses!" and put them on the dog, and give him a big treat.
- ❀ **Try on dark shades outdoors.** The manufacturer of Doggles warns that your dog won't think he can see if you try on dark glasses inside. "Imagine yourself wearing dark tinted glasses inside. You cannot see, and neither can your dog," they say. It makes sense to put the dark shades on your Joe Cool hound outside.
- ❀ **Take him cool places.** As soon as he's used to the new object, go places he likes. Take him to a friend's house and have them coo over his handsome new look. Go for a walk and have fun. Make wearing his headgear part of a happy life.
- ❀ **Repeat.** The more often you put on the glasses or hat, the better your dog will adjust. Practice at least three times a day, and your dog will soon assume that wearing a pair of shades is absolutely normal.

Remember fashion is about fun. Enjoy your dog, and know that all little dogs are naturally hip.

Goggles made just for dogs can protect his eyes, and look cool.

Section 2

The Spa Dog

Beauty isn't just about clothes, of course. It's even more about taking care of yourself. You wouldn't dress up in your favorite outfit without taking a bath and brushing your teeth first.

Dogs need to be clean, fresh-smelling, and well-groomed. They can learn to enjoy the spa treatment just as much as you like getting your hair and nails done. They can also enjoy the creature comforts, from massages to aromatherapy—and even the latest craze in hair color. It's all a matter of making it fun for your dog. This section will show you how!

Chapter 5

Hair, Glorious Hair!

Part of the charm of many little breeds is their fun, fabulous, fantastic fur. In fact, most little dogs have big hair. Sixteen of the twenty-one breeds in the toy group have at least some type of rough, tousled, or silky coat. Dogs like Yorkies, Poodles, and Maltese have  coats that grow continually, like human hair. Even "naked" Chinese Crested Dogs have a variety called a Powderpuff, who are covered with long, soft cottony coats.

If you have a long-haired breed (or mix), he desperately needs your help to keep him looking and feeling his best. Long hair mats, and mats hurt! When your dog has a mat on his tummy, it hurts to stretch out and sleep. If he has mats on his legs, it hurts to walk. Life is a nightmare for a dog with mats. Even human touch can be painful. Your dog might even start snapping at you, because he's in constant misery. You need to keep your dog combed, bathed, and trimmed so that he doesn't have to live this way.

Beware the Cotton Coat

Dog hair is usually described as harsh, silky, or cottony. The most difficult dogs to keep untangled are those with fluffy, soft, cottony coats like the Coton de Tulear or the Bichon Frise. Cottony coats can mat when a dog plays in the grass or roughhouses with one of his little buddies.

Dogs with cottony coats usually need short trims to deal with the constant mats. Also, talk with a professional groomer about conditioning products that might make the problem more manageable.

Glamour Coats: Long-Haired Dogs

The worst hair problems are with breeds who have coats that look highly exotic when they're perfectly groomed. These include Yorkies, Poodles, Shih Tzu, Lhasa Apsos, Maltese, Havanese, Bichon Frises, Coton de Tulear, plus other breeds and mixes who just happen to have hair that gets easily matted. If you have one of these breeds—or any dog with a long coat or a coat that mats easily—you need to give your dog's coat daily attention.

Even if your long-coated breed is trimmed into a short hairdo, these dogs absolutely require regular combing and shampooing. Remember that your dog is running, playing, digging, and going for walks in that hair. It's going to need daily attention.

Medium-Coated Dogs

Dogs with moderately long coats, and coats that don't tangle as much as long-haired dogs, include Papillons, Pomeranians, Cavalier King Charles Spaniels, and Long-Coated Chihuahuas, among others.

These breeds still need regular grooming—at least once a week—and many individuals need more than

An updo looks great with formal wear.

that. Look for problem areas where mats tend to form, such as the base of the ears, the area by your dog's elbows, and his tummy.

Short-Coated Dogs

Don't forget that your short-haired dog needs attention to his fur, too. A breed with a dense coat (like most Pugs), should be combed at least once a week. Even dogs with very short coats feel better when you stroke them all over with your hand. Combing and stroking help their circulation, and keep their coats shiny and glossy. You wouldn't want just the long-haired dogs to have healthy-looking hair!

The Low-Down on Undercoats

Dogs typically have two kinds of hair: an outer coat and an undercoat. The outer hair is harsh and protective. In winter, most breeds grow a soft, wooly undercoat that gives them warmth during the cold weather. When summer comes, the harsh outer coat actually insulates the dog from the summer sun and heat.

Dogs with an outer coat and an undercoat are called double-coated breeds. Examples of small double-coated breeds include Pomeranians and Pekingese. It's important to comb through the dense undercoat when you groom your double-coated dog. Otherwise, he can end up covered with one giant mat. It's

Long-Haired Dogs and Warm Winter Clothes

If you're looking for a sweater or jacket to keep your long-haired dog warm in winter, be sure to fit it so that it does more good than harm. Long-haired dogs, especially those with double coats, have their own insulation against the cold. The air in the insulating fur is warm, and protects your dog against the cold.

It's fine to dress your dog in a winter coat, but be sure that you don't squash his fur down tightly, eliminating that warm layer of air. If you do, he might be colder with his coat on than off. Winter clothes should leave plenty of room for that fur to do its job, and then the coat can keep your dog even more comfy.

A "Cling-on" Isn't a Star Wars Character

Combine long hair and a doggie's bodily functions, and you have the potential for a mess. In doggie circles, the result is known as a "cling-on." You've got to check your dog to be sure that poop isn't accumulating in his fur, since this is obviously a health hazard for your little dog. When you groom your dog, be sure to trim the hairs around his anus. This will reduce the likelihood of entanglements.

Teach your dog the command "Let me check." Start out by giving him a treat with one hand while your run a tissue or paper towel across his rump with the other. If you spot a "cling-on" remove it. (This may take combing out or a quick rinsing in the sink. After you rinse your dog, be sure to clean the sink with a disinfecting cleanser, such as a water–bleach mixture.) Your dog can get into a regular pattern of "Let me check" every time he comes inside from a potty break, keeping him clean and giving you a chance to keep on top of this potentially serious problem

You might want to trim around a male's penis and a female's vulva, so that there isn't an accumulation of urine and urine stains. Rinse off those areas regularly, as well.

Not every moment with your glamorous dog is a day at the beach, but both of you will appreciate your clean, happy, healthy, sweet-smelling little dog. It's just the way life is with a creature with long hair in intimate places!

important for his skin health to have air circulation, and that means combing down to the skin.

Some small breeds have wiry coats, including many of the terriers, such as West Highland White Terriers and Cairn Terriers. Show dogs with wiry coats are usually groomed by stripping out the undercoat with a special comb, leaving the harsh outer coat. Most pet terriers are not stripped, but trimmed with clippers, which leaves a soft-feeling coat. Why the coat change? It's because the soft undercoat grows out faster than the harsh, wiry outer coat.

Eventually, the harsh hairs will grow out again, and the original harsh feeling of the dog's fur will return.

Some breeds, including Yorkies, Papillons, and Silky Terriers, have single coats. Selective breeding has minimized the undercoats on these breeds.

Early Childhood Education

Start a grooming routine with your puppy as soon as he comes to your home. It takes several months for a dog's coat to achieve a long, flowing look, so use those months wisely. Brush and comb your puppy over every inch of his body. There won't be much hair to comb, and that's just what you want. If your pup gets used to combs and brushes before his coat gets long and likely to mat, he'll think grooming time is a delightful experience. It will never occur to him that it could be a struggle.

So, get out a soft brush and brush that puppy all over: his tummy, his feet, his tail, head. Wipe his face with a wash cloth. Give him treats, give him praise, tell him he's a little puppy genius. Do this now, and your life will be incomparably easier in the years ahead.

Brushing and Combing Your Diva

Whatever length your dog's coat is, brush and comb him at least once a week—more often if he has a coat that tends to mat. Some dogs, even in a short trim, need combing every day.

After brushing your dog, make sure you comb him to remove any remaining mats.

If you have a short-haired dog, you can use a grooming brush or a comb. If your little dog's hair is longer, start with a pin brush. Note: *Don't ever brush or comb a long-haired dog's coat when it is dry*—it will break his hair. Spritz his hair with a conditioning spray, then brush.

Gently brush your dog's entire body. Don't just brush the obvious areas, like the back and sides; gently brush the dog's tummy, the insides of his legs, and under his tail. It's those hidden places that are likely to develop the worst mats if you're not careful. If your dog has a long coat, brush one section at a time. Be sure you work clear down to the skin and not just brush on top of the hair, but be careful not to brush too hard and hurt his delicate skin.

Gentleness is the key. If you want your dog to like grooming, you can't jerk and tug. Be thorough, work through every hair on your dog, but do it gently, lovingly, and sweetly. Make this a happy time, not a frustrating, hurtful time.

Call for Help

It's easy for a dog's well-groomed coat to get quickly out of control, especially if you have a long-haired breed. One day your dog's coat looks great, and the next you can feel mats all over him. If you can't quickly and efficiently solve the problem for your little dog, call someone who can. A groomer has the equipment and experience to make the job easier. If your dog is severely matted, take him to your veterinarian to see if the best alternative is to anesthetize and shave him. Remember, his hair will grow back, and while it's growing it's a good time to practice your grooming routine so that the problem won't happen again.

After Brushing, Comb

After you've thoroughly brushed every inch of your dog, take a metal comb and comb every inch. You'll soon discover that brushes miss a lot of mats—especially the mats that are still small. Combing is not just for long-haired dogs. If your dog's coat is very dense, it can still mat even if it's short. For dogs with an undercoat, it's important to comb out the fur. However, there are some breeds just don't have enough hair to comb. (For example, most Italian

Greyhounds have very short, sleek coats and combing wouldn't be comfortable for them.)

Be especially careful when combing your dog's face. Brush out any bits of food that might have accumulated around your dog's mouth. If he has any discharge around his eyes, clean that up with a damp washcloth. Some people use a very fine-toothed comb, such as a flea comb, to carefully comb out any discharge that still remains near the eyes after it's been wiped off with a wash cloth.

Be very gentle combing around his ears—it is a sensitive

It's essential to get rid of painful mats.

area. But you must be vigilant about thoroughly combing behind your dog's ears, since the fine hair there is a prime place for mats to quickly accumulate. Also be very gentle when you're combing and brushing around your dog's genital area.

Tip for Removing Mats

Be careful if you're using scissors to cut out a mat, since most mats form right next to the skin. An old groomer's trick is to put a comb in between the mat and the skin, and work above the comb; that way, you know you can't accidentally nick your dog's skin.

When you're done, gently touch your dog all over. Do you feel any lumps or bumps? Is he feeling a little thin, or do you have a portly pooch? Your regular grooming sessions with your dog are a great time to do a little health check and catch potential problems long before they turn into crises.

While you're grooming, talk sweetly and happily to your dog. Some people sing. Tell him he's handsome, that you love him, and that he's gorgeous. Make grooming time the highlight of the day—something you both truly enjoy.

Muttering Over Mat Matters

Your little dog is more than capable of creating mats on his own. Unfortunately, humans often add to the problem. If you have a long-haired dog, especially one with a cottony coat—do not rub your hands back and forth in his coat! "We see so many mats around the faces of little, long-haired dogs," says one groomer. "It's people scratching the dog's ears, neck, and face." Remember, mats cause misery; pet long-haired dogs along with flow of the hair, not against it. This will help prevent mats from forming.

Surprisingly, another top time for mat creation is in the bath. (Think of them as "bath mats!") Do not scrub your dog's hair back and forth when you bathe him! Just massage gently, going with the direction of the hair.

Removing Mats

If you find a mat when brushing your little guy, hold the hair above the mat, and work the mat out with the brush (or your comb). If combing the mat out hurts your dog, snip it out with your scissors (unless you are planning to show your dog). Your dog's hair will grow back in sooner or later, and no mat is worth causing your dog pain.

Times to Pay Special Attention to Coats

There are times when even coats considered "wash and wear" will cause you trouble. Plan ahead to pay special attention during these times.

When the Puppy Coat Sheds

At about 4 months of age, your little guy will lose that fuzzy puppy coat and begin to grow in his grown-up fur. The shedding fur and the new hair often get tangled into a mess. Brush your pup every day during this time. It will catch the shedding hairs before they tangle, and it will help your dog to learn that grooming is part of his daily routine.

At About 9 Months

Many breeds begin to have the appearance of their adult coats when the pups are about 9 months old. Suddenly, your dog's hair is long enough to really tangle, when it wasn't before. Keep a daily eye on your dog when his coat begins to reach adult length, or you'll find yourself cutting out big pieces of it that are hopelessly snarled mats.

Spring and Autumn

It's probably no surprise that, when your dog sheds in the spring, he's likely to become matted. Of course, it's crucial to comb him out as often as necessary (and that might be daily) in spring. What might surprise you is that autumn, when your dog is growing his winter coat, is also a big time for mats to form. It's important to keep the coat groomed during this time, or you'll face tangles.

Sprays and Spritzes

The rule for all long-haired dogs is to never, ever brush a dry coat, because it will break off those beautiful hairs. Instead, spray just a bit of moisture on the dog before you brush. Most people simply use water.

However, a cadre of fanciers have their own potions they like to spray and

Never brush a long-haired dog's coat when it is dry—spray on a bit of water before you begin.

Summer Cuts

Be sure that your dog's summer 'do isn't too short. A dog who's shaved to the skin can get sunburned. A modest amount of hair can actually help insulate your dog against the summer sun and heat.

spritz on their dogs to give the coats a fabulous glimmer. Much like choosing a shampoo, the only way to choose a good moisturizing spray is by trial and error. If it is scented, make sure both you and your dog think it's pleasant.

Some spritzes, like the Cain & Able line, include essential oils such as citronella, eucalyptus, and lavender, which are natural insect repellants. I must say I thought my dogs wouldn't like those scents, but they do. (And as a bonus, they smell good to humans, too.)

Tying the Topknot

Some of the small breeds with long hair, like Yorkies, traditionally have the hair around their face pulled into a topknot. It makes sense, since it's important to keep stray hairs out of your little dog's eyes. When novices first attempt the topknot, it can end up looking more like Pebbles Flintstone than Cindy Crawford (more like a little palm tree than a sophisticated 'do).

The secret to a great topknot is back-combing. Yes, you need to tease your dog's hair to get the cool poof of fur. Here's how to do it.

- Gather the hair from above his eyes to the crown of his head and comb it out.
- Gently back-comb the hair to add volume.
- Secure the topknot with a latex band.
- Smooth over the back-combed area so that it appears smooth, but still has the shape and volume of a fancy topknot.
- Tie a bow around the latex band.

With a little practice, and fine-tuning the technique for your dog, you'll have a fancy topknot. A cool alternative to the bow: Braid the topknot, giving a cool, kicky look to your hipster hound.

What's the secret to a great topknot? Backcombing!

Rows and Floes of Ribbons

Long-haired dogs look fabulous in ribbons. Grooming supply companies sell bows that are attached to barrettes and rubber bands, to make it easier to put them in.

If you're looking for different and interesting ribbons, check out your local craft and fabric stores. The length you'll need for a bow will cost you just pennies, and you can get fabulous colors and textures that you don't usually find in ribbons marketed for dogs.

Finding Your Inner Pink Poodle

The 1950s were a strange and even frightening time in America: Cars had huge fins; cool guys wore greasy duck-tailed hair cuts and loafers; science fiction movies like The *Attack of the Killer Tomatoes* were box office hits. But nothing was stranger than the sight of a woman in an enormous pink bouffant

hairdo carrying a Toy Poodle with his own pink bouffant hair.

Just when you thought it was safe to go outside (eerie music should play here), the pink Poodle is back. And the purple Maltese. And the red, white, and blue Bichon.

Luckily for our little dogs, the old, harsh chemical dyes of the 1950s are gone. In their place are vegetable dyes that won't hurt your dog or damage his coat. So, if you're in the mood, why not let him be gloriously colorful for a few months? And maybe you'll want to dye your hair purple to match. Just promise—no bouffants!

Everyone has a inner pink Poodle dying to get out.

Chapter 6

"Bath" Doesn't Have to Be a Four-Letter Word

Well, okay, for those of us who were English majors, technically "bath" *is* a four-letter word. But it doesn't have to be a bad word. You can and should make bath time a relaxed and even pleasant time for your small dog.

The Basics: Before You Bathe
Comb Out Your Dog

Rule Number One: Always thoroughly brush and comb your long-haired dog before you bathe him. If your dog has any mats in his hair when he gets wet, they will become extremely difficult to get out. Yes, you'll have to brush your dog, bathe him, and brush him again. That may sound like a lot of work, but it's much less work than trying to get the mats out once they're set in by a bath.

Have Your Supplies Ready

Before you start, get organized. The last thing you want is a wriggling little wet dog under your arm while you're wandering through the house looking for a towel.

You'll need:

- ❈ Nonskid mat and filter in the sink
- ❈ Spray nozzle for the faucet (if your sink doesn't have a spray attachment)
- ❈ Shampoo
- ❈ Conditioner
- ❈ Towels
- ❈ Blow dryer
- ❈ Comb
- ❈ Pin brush (for long-haired breeds)
- ❈ Blunt-edged scissors to trim feet and tidy up coat (for long-haired breeds)

As cute as he looks in a bath, a "shower" is a better option.

Technically, It's a Shower, Not a Bath

It's cute to see photos of a dog in a tub full of suds. But in real life, you don't want your dog sitting in a tub of dirty water. Dogs need showers, not baths. It's uncomfortable, unwieldy, and inefficient to bathe your dog in even an inch of water. It should all go down the drain.

Use the spray attachment on your faucet to wet down your dog.

Most of us bathe our little guys in the sink, since it's easy and convenient. Be sure to put a nonskid mat in the bottom of the sink—your dog will be calmer and more comfortable with sure footing. You can cut down an inexpensive rubber bath mat bought at the grocery store. Do be sure to put a filter over the drain—you don't want a little paw going down the garbage disposal! (If your sink doesn't have a filter, you can purchase one very inexpensively at the grocery store.)

You'll want a spray attachment for rinsing your dog. If you have an old-fashioned sink that doesn't have a spray attachment, you can purchase one at a pet supply stores; these spray attachments fit over the faucet and work just fine.

Be sure the water temperature feels just slightly warm on your skin. Your little dog has very sensitive skin, and it hurts if the water is too warm, and it isn't any fun if the water is too cold. Have the water running before you put your dog in the sink, so he doesn't have to wait and worry while you fiddle with the water temperature.

The Zen of Bathing

No matter how weird and wacky your dog becomes, stay calm and gentle. Don't rush, don't get frustrated. If you get upset, your dog will be more wriggly and difficult. Run water over his coat to get it wet, gently massage in the shampoo, and then work the conditioner into his hair.

When the shampoo and conditioner have been thoroughly massaged on all parts of the dog, rinse thoroughly. Then rinse again. And again. And one more time for good measure. (Aren't you glad you have that hose attachment on the sink?) Be sure to rinse the spots you might forget, including your dog's tummy, personal parts, and tail. Nothing can cause more irritation to your dog's skin—and make his coat look more dull—than shampoo that didn't get rinsed out.

Be very careful when you're washing your little guy's head and face, especially around his eyes. You might want to look for a "no tears" shampoo so that you don't have to worry about getting soap in your dog's eyes. Rinse very gently around the dog's head.

After he's thoroughly rinsed (you're sure he's thoroughly rinsed, right?), it's time to dry him. Be sure that where you dry him has a towel or mat down for solid footing. Start by completely towel-drying your little guy. Hold and gently squeeze him, rather than rubbing—remember, you don't want to create mats!

Comb out his hair, being sure to get out any tangles at his elbows, behind his ears, on his tummy—all the places that are easy to overlook. If it's a warm summer day, or if you have a short-haired dog, it might be fine to just let your dog air dry the rest of the way. However, most of the time, you'll also want to blow dry your dog. It's best if you use a dryer

Be Careful!

Little dogs have delicate bones. If your guy takes a flying leap from the counter, he could break his leg or worse. If he's wriggly, you might want to start out washing him in the bathtub. Of course, you must never, ever leave your dog unattended for a single second on a countertop or other high place. If you realize you forgot to put your brush on the counter, pick up your wet dog, and carry him with you while you look for the brush. You would never forgive yourself if he hurt himself because you turned your eyes away.

specifically designed for dogs (there's at least one brand that's a portable little dryer that sits on your counter and leaves your hands free). You can also find stands in which to place human hair dryers that will leave your hands free to groom your dog, which is always a good idea.

If you're using a human dryer, be sure to set the temperature on the lowest setting. Your dog's skin is very sensitive, and a hot dryer will hurt. Keep the volume on "low" as well—the air at full blast will practically blow a little guy off the counter.

Those Darn Mats!

Long-haired dogs have a constant battle with mats. One of the worst culprits in creating mats? The bath! Never "scrub" your long-haired dog's hair in the bath—it creates mats at an alarming rate. Just gently run your fingers through the coat, and squeeze water out with your hand. No rubbing on that tangle-prone coat!

BAD HAIR DAY

Remember, your dog's hair will flow in the direction the dryer is pointed. Gently brush the way your want the coat to go as you dry the hair. All the while, tell your dog he's wonderful, and gorgeous, and that time with a dryer is worth it. He'll soon learn that it's just part of being beautiful.

TIP: After a bath, it's common for dogs to need to pee. I have no idea why, but they do. As soon as you've dried your little guy, take him out for a

Rinse out the shampoo, then rinse again!

quick potty break to avoid a "housebreaking indiscretion."

How Often?

There isn't a rule about how often to bathe—or not bathe—your dog. Unlike humans, dogs don't sweat. So, despite people's perceptions of "doggie odor," they generally accumulate bad odors a lot slower than humans do.

Some dogs tend to be oily, and need to be bathed every week or two. Others can go several weeks without a bath. If you're using good-quality products, and giving your dog a healthy diet that keeps his skin supple, most dogs can be bathed weekly without any harm.

Shampoos and Conditioners

There's no one "best" shampoo or conditioner for a dog. Every dog's skin and hair are different. Experiment, just as you do for your own hair, until you find products that you and your dog like.

Do look for formulas that are gentle. Products

What Not to Wear

Don't use a human shampoo on your dog. Most "people" shampoos will leave your dog's skin dry, itchy, and flaking. Even breeds like Yorkies, that have hair very much like a human's, need dog shampoos and conditioners, because their skin and coat have a dog's chemical balance.

With patience and some tasty treats, you can get your little dog used to the dryer.

76

for sensitive skin are always a good choice, since all dogs have sensitive skin. Plus, little dogs are usually bathed more often than big dogs.

I like shopping for shampoo with my dogs, so I can be sure they like the smell. After all, what smells good to us humans often smells pretty awful to a dog. (And, of course, we all know of things that dogs think smell wonderful that we find icky!) If my dog turns

Getting Used to the Dryer

Hair dryers are noisy and windy. It's no surprise that lots of dogs find them scary. If your dog is afraid of the dryer, try to give him a new association with the dryer. Leave it in plain sight—and reward your dog when he's near it. Scratch your dog's chest and hold the dryer in one hand. Show him the dryer isn't going to eat him! Once the sight of the dryer doesn't scare him, turn the dryer on while your dog is across the room. Reward your dog with a treat, and gradually work closer and closer to the dryer, always with fun and treats—never forcing him. Be patient, take your time, and soon you'll have a dog who loves the hair dryer, because good things always happen when he's near it.

his head and grimaces when I put the product down for him to sniff, we buy something else.

It only makes sense to look for products that have as many natural ingredients as possible. The fewer weird and unpronounceable chemicals that come into contact with your dog's skin, the better.

Most dogs also benefit from a conditioner formulated for dogs, not humans. That's especially important for long-haired dogs, since it keeps tangling to a minimum.

Places to Find Great Shampoos and Conditioners

✳ **Your Veterinarian's Office.** Most veterinarians carry shampoo in their clinics. It usually doesn't look very fancy, but most of these products are great. They are usually specially formulated for dogs with sensitive skin (and frequent bathers). My veterinarian carries an aloe and oatmeal shampoo that allows me to skip the conditioner on my Papillons.

✳ **Pet Boutiques.** Retail and online stores have some products that are sumptuous. The latest trend is shampoo that contains essential oils. (Essential oils are used in aromatherapy to promote health benefits.) Some contain ingredients such as citronella, eucalyptus, and lavender, which can help to repel bugs.

❉ **Groomers.** Many groomers sell premium shampoos that they use in their establishment. Groomers are usually up-to-date on the best new products, and often can give you a lot of help in finding the right choice for your particular pet.

❉ **Pet Supply Stores.** The large chain stores usually have a wide variety of pet shampoos. Bring your dog with you to help select one that smells good to both of you, and remember to look for one with as many natural ingredients as possible.

Where Not to Buy

Most grocery stores only carry pet shampoos that are full of chemicals and will dry out your pet's hair. Unless you have a grocery store that is carrying premium shampoos, go to your veterinarian, pet boutique, groomer, or pet supply store.

After the Bath

When he's shampooed and conditioned, toweldried and blow-dried, tell your dog just how fabulous he looks! It will make him feel happy. Then go have an adventure together. Life should be fun, as well as glamorous, for your little dog!

Chapter 7

Putting Your Best Foot Forward: From Pet-icures to Buying the Right Boots

There's something magical about dog paws, and that magic is only magnified when those paws are tiny. When paws are clean and healthy, they smell sweet and a little bit like pine. The bottom of a dog's paw is bare skin, much like a human hand. When we touch that surface, a special closeness forms between dog and human…unless your dog is biting, hiding, and running from you. Or his feet hurt. It's important for you to take care of your little guy's feet.

This chapter talks about taking care of those wonderful feet and toes, from the basics to the not-so basic—from trimming toenails to selecting the right nail polish and boots.

Foot Care Basics

You know how awful you feel when your feet hurt. The pain in your feet inevitable expands to your back, and then to your head, and you end up with a pounding headache. The same is true for your dog.

Sadly, it's more than likely that most dogs have paws that hurt them.

Hair and Nails Grow at Different Rates

Many toy dogs such as Poodles, Shih Tzu, and Yorkies go to the groomer regularly for haircuts. Of course, nail trimming is usually part of this regular grooming. That may lull you into a false sense of security when it comes to your dog's nails. While most dogs get their hair cut about every 6 weeks, most nails need to be trimmed every 2 to 4 weeks.

Talk with your groomer about whether your dog would benefit from extra nail trimming between grooming visits. You can do the nails yourself, or bring your dog back to his groomer.

Why? Because their toenails are too long. If you can hear your dog's nails clicking when he walks, that means with every step he takes, his nails are pushing against his feet, which hurts his toes. When nails get too long, it can create permanent damage to his legs and can cause back pain.

It's important to trim your dog's nails regularly. How often depends on how much your dog walks on surfaces such as sidewalks that wear down nails, and

Keep your pup's feet looking fine.

also on how fast his nails happen to grow. For some dogs, that might be as little as once a month; for others, trimming might be required more frequently. The rule of thumb is: If you hear the dog's nails click when he walks, his nails are too long.

Your dog needs to have his feet checked daily, and his nails trimmed regularly. Don't think of it as a difficult task—think of it as giving your dog a "pet-icure."

Put Your Little Foot Right Here

The most important step in caring for your dog's precious paws is getting your little guy used to having his feet handled. Most people simply grab their dog's paw and start trimming. That's where all the trouble starts.

A dog's instinct tells him that it's dangerous to let anyone grab his foot. Your little Chihuahua or Pekingese might not look much like a wolf, but his brain is still wired like his ancestor's. If something happens to a wolf's feet, he can't hunt, and wouldn't make it in the wild for long. It's normal and natural for dogs to resist someone grabbing their feet and fiddling with their paws— the canine brain perceives it as deadly. It's amazing that any dogs' nails get trimmed!

Happily, your dog can be counterconditioned against their instincts and learn to enjoy having his feet held and massaged, which will help him easily tolerate nail trimming. All it takes is a little food and a bit of patience on your part.

Treat When You Trim!

The object is to make foot handling and nail trimming a relaxed part of a happy routine. So, give your dog treats when you are working with his feet. Tell him he's grand, and make it a good time for him. Treats will help him understand you're not punishing him for something!

Teaching Your Dog to Accept Foot Handling

Here's what to do:

- Determine your dog's tolerance for having his feet touched. Does he pull back at your hand coming near him, or does he accept your holding his paw in your hand? (What feels comfortable to him will depend on his past experiences and on how sensitive his feet are. Some breeds, such as Corgis, have notoriously sensitive feet.)

Touch his foot at the level that's comfortable for him and give him a treat. Attach a word to the act of touching his foot. I say, "Toes!" My dogs know I'm going to touch their feet—and they'll get a treat for it—when I say, "Toes!"

 Find a position that's comfortable for both of you. Some dogs like to lie on their backs. Others want to stand upright and offer one paw at a time. Some people prefer having the dogs on their laps, while others prefer a grooming table. Work out what's best for you and your dog. If you have more than one dog, your different dogs might prefer different positions.

 Build up gradually the amount you touch your dog's foot. Begin to hold the paw for a few seconds at a time. If he pulls away, move your hand with his paw, so you're never pulling at his foot. (You don't want to play tug-of-war with his toes!)

 Eventually, you can give your dog little foot massages. He'll learn that having his feet touched, stroked, and held by you is safe, comfortable, and fun.

 At first, don't even consider trimming his nails. If his nails need to be trimmed before he's comfortable having his feet held, take him to a groomer or to your veterinarian for the job. Let someone else be the bad guy, until he's more relaxed with having his feet touched.

After your dog accepts having his feet handled, you must be consistent. Feel all four paws every day. Check between his pads for things that get stuck—from bubble gum to pebbles. Check his nails and the bottoms of his pads for any injuries or splits (little dogs can injure their little feet just as easily a big dogs can injure theirs). Gently massage your dog's feet. Sing him a little song. You'll both feel good, and you'll both enjoy your little dog's pet-icure.

Nail Trimming 101

For most toy-sized dogs, cat nail clippers work wonderfully. They're small and, for most people, easier to control than the guillotine-style nail clippers. Dogs on the larger end of the scale, such as Westies or Cavalier King Charles Spaniels, have thicker nails. For those dogs, traditional dog nail trimmers work best.

Another option for your little guy is an electronic nail grinder. This device uses a rotating sandpaper end to groom the nails without the danger of cutting past the quick (the nerve and blood vessel that runs through your dog's nail) and causing bleeding. If the dog is sensitive to noise or has long hair (which may get wrapped up in the rotating grinder end), a nail clipper is a better alternative.

Pedicures are important! Keep your little dog's nails trimmed.

How to Trim Your Dog's Nails

Once your dog is comfortable with you touching and holding his feet, you can begin training him to accept nail trimming. Start by holding the nail clippers next to his foot, and rewarding him with a treat. When he's used to the clippers, trim just one toenail, give him a treat, and call it a day. A day or two later, trim another nail. Over time, work up to trimming all the nails on the same day.

When you cut the nails, just trim the very tips of the nails: You don't want to hit the quick and cause bleeding. It can be challenging to keep from nicking the quick on dogs with black nails. If your dog has at least one light-colored nail, use that as a guide, and only snip back as far as you can on the light-colored nail. If all the dog's nails are black, snip tiny amounts, and watch to be sure that your dog isn't feeling any discomfort.

If you work slowly and carefully, there is no reason to ever nick the quick and make your dog bleed. If you do accidentally cut the quick, just hold the end of your dog's nail against the tip of your finger to stop the bleeding, or use a styptic pen or powder.

If your dog's nails are very long, don't try cut too much nail all at

Relax!

When you trim your dog's nails, remember to keep your hand and body relaxed. Breathe! If you're tense, your dog will pick up on your mood, and he'll be afraid.

Remember the Dewclaws!

Don't forget to trim the nails on your little guy's dewclaws, if he has them. (Dewclaws are the little "thumbs" located on your dog's ankles.) These nails grow very quickly, because they don't receive any wear. If left untrimmed, they can grow into your dog's skin. Regularly checking and trimming your dog's dewclaws isn't hard to do, and it's very important.

once. The quick grows with the nail, and if you cut too much from a long nail, your more likely to hit the quick. Just trim a little bit each week for over-long nails. Over time, the quick inside your dog's nail will retreat, and your little guy will soon enjoy the comfortable feeling that comes with well-trimmed nails.

Finishing Touch

If you're using a nail clipper, the nail is sometimes left sharper than before you cut your it. Finish off his nail treatment by filing the tips of his nails to a rounded point. For little dogs, an emery board from the cosmetics section of the drug store will do fine. That finishing touch will make it pleasant to carry your dog in your arms, even right after his nail trim, because no jagged pieces will be left to get caught on anything.

High-five for picture-perfect feet.

Trimming Hairy Paws

If you have a long-haired breed, don't forget to trim the hair between the pads of your dog's feet. This hair can grow very quickly, especially if your dog doesn't often walk on sidewalks or other rough surfaces. When you trim your dog's nails, check out his feet. Using a pair of blunt-nosed scissors, snip away excess hair from the bottom of the foot. You can also tidy up the sides of the feet.

A Little Polish for Your Princess?

You should be proud—you're taking great care of your dog's little feet. The nails are trimmed, the hair is short on her pads. She just needs one more thing to be the picture of elegance: Nail polish, of course.

Check out Color Paw, a premium pet nail polish. The product covers the nail in a single coat, and dries in about 20 seconds. Quick drying action is essential for "paw-lish"—you don't want a dog with wet nails running around the house.

Most people simply let their dog's polish wear off. Or, you can remove it with nail polish remover that doesn't have acetone in its formula. You must be sure to wash your dog's feet after using nail polish remover.

Nail polish can be a fun fashion statement for your little diva—it's especially noticeable on short-haired dogs.

Perfectly manicured feet are beautiful and practical.

It's Okay to Call in a Trained Professional

If you have a wriggly puppy, or the thought of cutting your little dog's nails sends you into fits of worry, relax. Take your little guy into a groomer or to your veterinarian's office and ask a trained professional to do the job. In most parts of the country, a quick nail trim with a cooperative dogs won't cost much, and it will be money well spent.

These Boots Were Made for (Dog) Walking

Now that you know how to keep your dog's tootsies looking and feeling their best. To keep them that way, think about protecting them during winter walks—think about boots.

If you think that only little fru-fru dogs wear boots, think again. Booties are required equipment for dogs that run the Iditarod sled race (eight booties per dog must be brought along on the race). Mushers know that icy conditions are hard on their dogs' feet, and most protect their feet with boots.

Okay, you aren't going to strap your Chihuahua to a sled and ask him to pull you from Anchorage to Nome in the dead of winter. But if you live in a cold climate, you will be asking your dog to walk in cold conditions. City sidewalks have salt and chemical de-icers that can burn your dog's paws. The bottom

Get along little doggie! Once your dog is acclimated to footwear, the sky's the limit for fashion and fun.

line: Boots can be just as practical for your little Pomeranian as they are for the Alaskan Huskies who are running the race.

You have choices that those Alaskan dogs can only dream about! Little Lily makes Lilyboots, in styles that look like go-go boots, tennis shoes, or fur shearlings. All these boots are zipped up and Velcroed, making a secure fit. If your dog does serious exercise, such as jogging, or if he regularly walks on rougher surfaces, you might want to purchase booties from Ruff Wear—these boots are preferred by many search-and-rescue dogs.

Before buying boots for you dog, it's a good idea to try them on your little dog (if you can) to make sure they fit. Does your dog's paw fit in the foot area comfortably? Does the boot stay on his leg securely? If you can't try boots on, some online retailers have pawprint sizing, so that you can match your dog's foot to the right size shoe before you order.

Seasonal Foot Care

If Your Dog Is Barefoot in Winter…
Remember to rinse his feet off every time he comes in from a walk. You don't want him licking off the salt and chemicals that have been placed on the sidewalk for de-icing.

If Your Dog Is Barefoot in Summer…
Remember, sidewalks and streets get hot! Put you hand on the sidewalk. If it's uncomfortable, carry your dog. That's a great day to be thankful that you have an 8-pound (3.6 kg) Miniature Pinscher instead of an 80-pound (36.3 kg) Doberman Pinscher!

Acclimate Your Dog to Boots

If a canine brain thinks nail-trimming is scary, think how odd it must consider a pair of boots. Use the same techniques outlined earlier for nail-trimming to get your dog used to having his feet handled, which includes giving him rewards when you put the boots on.

When you've done all this great care for your dog's feet, he'll feel great. Believe it or not, if you follow the methods in this chapter, your dog actually will feel more bonded to you than ever before. Plus, he'll look fab from the feet up!

Chapter 8

Groomers: When It's Time to Call in the Professionals

I'm guessing you probably haven't tried to cut your own hair since you were about six. You know that the odds of getting a great-looking hairdo the "do-it-yourself" way are probably about as good now as they were back then. Many people attempt to cut their dog's hair with equally disastrous results. Sometimes, the best thing to do is to call in a trained professional.

Many of the most popular little dogs are all about the hair. Poodles, Bichon Frises, Shih Tzu, Maltese, Lhasa Apsos, and Yorkies all have coats that grow continuously—just like human hair does. Every 6 weeks or so, these little guys need a haircut. For these breeds, most people turn to a professional groomer. One groomer explains the need for a professional touch this way: "Owners only practice on their dogs once a month or so, but I am grooming dogs every day."

Finding a Great Groomer

Groomers aren't required to have any special training or certification—most are self-taught. As a result, the abilities and professionalism in the field range widely. You'll need to do your homework to find just the right groomer for your dog.

To find a great groomer, ask around. Your veterinarian can probably recommend one. In fact, many veterinary clinics have groomers working for them, and most others know local groomers in the area who are professional, safe, and reliable.

If you purchased your puppy from a breeder, she also may be able to help. If your breeder competes in dog shows, she'll probably know someone in your area with the same breed, or a breed that needs similar grooming, and she may connect you with a good groomer.

Sometimes, the answer is walking on four well-manicured paws in your neighborhood. If you see someone whose dog has a great 'do, ask them where they go for grooming. The person with that well-coifed canine will probably be awfully glad you noticed how excellent her dog looks, and will be glad to give you a referral.

A hairstyle like this doesn't happen overnight.

You'll want to meet the groomer before you leave your dog with her. See how she communicates with you and how she relates to your dog. If you don't like the feel of the place, go someplace else.

Whether you end up someplace famous, like Manhattan's Doggie-Do and Pussycats Too! (where, rumor has it, Jennifer Lopez and Puff Daddy's dogs go) or to somewhere in your neighborhood, you're still looking for the same thing:

loving, gentle, competent care that leaves your dog looking terrific.

Finding the Best Groomer for Your Breed

Do you have a breed with specialized grooming requirements? Poodles and Bichon Frises, for example, require a lot of sculpting of fur, and Poodles require careful shaving of their feet in most trims. If you want your Poodle to look like a Poodle, or your Bichon to look like a Bichon, you need someone who is experienced in working with those breeds. The problem can be finding someone who truly knows what she's doing with breeds that need specialized grooming.

Find a groomer both you and your dog are comfortable with.

One groomer recommends asking the open-ended question, "Do you have any breeds you specialize in?" Explains the groomer, "If you call someone up and say, 'Do you know how to groom a Poodle?' she'll probably say she does. But, if you call and ask what breeds she specializes in, and she names several and a Poodle isn't on the list, that might not be the groomer you're looking for."

Four Things You Should Expect from a Groomer

- **Safety.** Most grooming is done on a grooming table with your dog held in place using a collar around his neck. The groomer's tools of the trade are sharp scissors that can be dangerous in careless hands. Your dog deserves someone who has safety as her top priority.

- **Kindness.** Many dogs are scared of the groomer, they and may respond to the stress of the situation with growls, nips, and even serious bites. Some groomers respond by being too tough with dogs. Don't even think about leaving a dog with someone you suspect slaps, pinches, or manhandles your dog.

- **Knowledge of the Breed and the Cuts.** Each breed has its standard cuts.

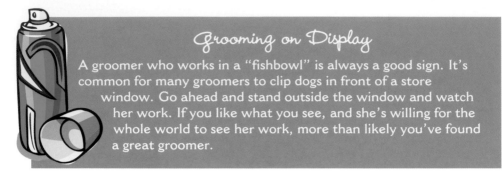

Grooming on Display

A groomer who works in a "fishbowl" is always a good sign. It's common for many groomers to clip dogs in front of a store window. Go ahead and stand outside the window and watch her work. If you like what you see, and she's willing for the whole world to see her work, more than likely you've found a great groomer.

Your Yorkie won't look like a Yorkie if he's trimmed, blow-dried, and combed like a Shih Tzu.

Communication. You and the groomer must be able to talk. She must not only understand how you want your dog to look, but she must relay any problems she might have had grooming your little guy. A good groomer will ask plenty of questions to find what works for you. All great groomers are also great communicators.

Four Things Your Groomer Should Expect from You

Honesty. Most of use have heard the big lies: "The check is in the mail" and "I'll still respect you in the morning"; for a groomer, the big one they hear all the time is, "Oh no, he won't bite." If you have a dog that's likely to snap when someone tries to trim his toenails or clean his ears, you must tell the groomer. This can be a difficult and even dangerous profession—it's not fair to make it harder by not telling the truth

Don't be afraid to call in a professional groomer, especially for a breed with a high-maintenance coat.

about your dog. An experienced groomer can usually work with a dog that has issues, as long as she is forewarned. She'll cradle the dog in her arm while she trims, or calmly put on a soft muzzle so that he can't bite. What groomers resent is not having these chances to protect themselves.

🌷 **A Dog who isn't Full of Mats.** Mats hurt. Groomers routinely see animals that are so badly matted that every step is painful. The loving families of these dogs often have no idea that they're hurting their dog. You comb your hair between visits to the hairdresser, and your dog's coat needs to be combed and brushed between trips to the groomer. If that doesn't work for you, take him in for a weekly touch-up. Don't wait 4 or 6 weeks and bring a matted dog into the grooming salon. It's cruel to your dog. We'll explain how to comb out your dog between baths in the next chapter.

🌷 **Clear Expectations.** If you want something, tell the groomer. For example, you might be envisioning a certain kind of trim for your Poodle, but there are several types of routine Poodle cuts. She doesn't know which one you want

Reality Check

Photos make a good starting point to discussing a style for your dog. However, sometimes both humans and dogs don't always meet the expectations created by those photos. Years ago, I worked in a large office area. One of the women who worked with me was short, plump, and dark-haired. She went off on her lunch break one day to get a Farrah Fawcett-style 'do, which was quite the fashion at the time. She came back from the appointment very upset: Despite having spent her money on that haircut, she still didn't look a bit like blonde, leggy actress Farrah Fawcett.

So, even with a fabulous groomer, your little guy might not look exactly like that Westminster Kennel Club dog show winner whose picture you keep lovingly in your wallet.

Your pet might not be the same shape as the dog in the photo. Perhaps he's portly, and may not have the sleek outline of the dog model. Hours of effort by the groomer can't change his basic physique.

Sometimes, the looks you see in magazines or at dog shows can be hard to maintain. Listen to the groomer's ideas about ways to achieve a similar look that might be easier to keep clean and combed.

unless you tell her. Close shaves or hair left longer, whiskers on or whiskers trimmed, puffy tail or elegant shaping—you'd be amazed at the choices in dog grooming. Explain as clearly as you can what you want. Just as it can help your human hairdresser if you bring in a photo or two with styles that you like, it can help the groomer if you bring a photo of a dog with the hair you dream of for your dog.

🌷 **Respect.** This is a hard job. It includes animal behavior knowledge, artistry, and heavy lifting. A person who does this work well, and makes your animal look and feel good, deserves your respect.

Why Can't I Stay with My Little Dog When He's Being Groomed?

If you hang around a good grooming salon for a morning, you'll see worried people leaving their dogs with the groomer. The humans cry, the dogs shake and look at their people with sad eyes. Then the dog's family leaves, and the dog calmly accepts the competent hands of the groomer.

Most often, grooming is harder for the dog when his human stays with him. He doesn't have the chance to bond with the groomer and relax in her expert care. Here are some tips to make the grooming experience easier for both of you.

Don't Create a Scene

Of course it's hard to leave your baby behind, but you owe it to your dog to make the grooming process as easy as possible for him. That means no tears, and no holding on to the dog with fingers so tight that your knuckles are

Just Say "No" to Drugs

If your groomer wants to use tranquilizers or other drugs on your dog, this should be a big, flashing warning sign that something isn't right. Do not even consider leaving a dog with someone who does this! Drugs of any kind should never, ever be given to a dog, except under a veterinarian's supervision. Period.

If you have a dog that is very badly matted, talk with your veterinarian. He may recommend putting your dog under anesthesia and shaving the mats out. Putting a dog under anesthesia must be done at a veterinarian's office.

Worse than Crazy Hair Magazines....

You've seen those hair magazines in your hair stylist's shop. They show the latest styles, and sometimes models from hairstyle competition winners. And the hair is usually so wacky looking that you'd threaten to sue your stylist if your hair ever ended up like that. (I've always been convinced that hair dressers have those magazines in their shops so that we feel grateful with whatever style they give us, because it will certainly look better than what's in the book.)

Well, human hair stylists have nothing on weird dog hair. Grooming competitions usually include a creative class where a patient Poodle is dolled up in ways unimaginable, like being clipped in the shape of a fish and dyed blue to look tropical. Of course, the groomer wears a matching mermaid outfit.

turning white while the groomer pries your little dog away. And it definitely means not saying, "Oh my poor little darling. I am so, so sorry. I can't believe I'm deserting you in this terrible place with the mean lady!" The more distraught you are, the more frightened your dog will be. If you don't trust the groomer, don't leave your dog with her. If you do trust the groomer, help your dog do the same.

To help keep your dog calm, develop a phrase that you use whenever you're going to be leaving your dog, whether it's when you go to work in the morning or when you're leaving him at the groomer. In the same calm, peaceful voice, simply say, "I'll be back" (or whatever phrase you prefer) and calmly leave.

When you return, greet your dog, happily tell him he looks fabulous, but don't act as if you're rescuing him from prison. Be happy, be warm—but be relaxed. It will make him feel more confident next time.

The Groom-Mobile

If you don't want to leave your dog at the groomer, consider bringing the groomer to your dog. Mobile grooming shops basically bring the spa to you—a rig complete with tubs and all the grooming equipment. This option costs a bit more, since the groomer has to make up for driving time. Still, it's a great option for a shy or worried dog. He knows that he's just a step away from home.

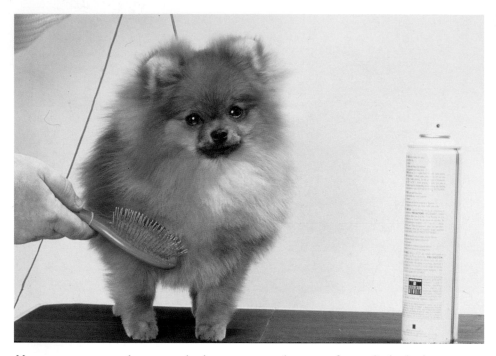

Your groomer can show you the best way to take care of your little dog's coat.

Asking Your Groomer for Help

A lot of people think it's great fun to groom their own dog. If you want to try it—go for it! Lots of dedicated amateurs have dogs with professional-looking 'dos. Even if your dog doesn't end up looking so terrific, it's not the end of the world. Hair grows back on dogs, just as it does on people.

To learn more about grooming your dog, ask your groomer if she'll teach you how to do it. You might be surprised that most groomers are glad to give lessons to their clients. One of those groomers admits an ulterior motive. "When I start showing them what it takes to groom a dog, most people realize how hard my job is and decide they want no part of it. I had one woman give up after she'd done one and-and-a-half paws." Still, whether you learn to groom your dog or just learn to admire your groomer, a hands-on lesson from a groomer will help you do a good job for your little dog.

Chapter 9

Beauty Secrets of Show Dogs

I can guess what you do the second week of February—you're sitting on the couch, glued to the TV, watching the Westminster Kennel Club dog show. Who doesn't love watching those glorious dogs strutting before the cheering crowds at Madison Square Garden like fashion models on a runway?

And just like fashion models, show dogs have to stick to a strict regimen of beauty care. Learn their beauty secrets, and your petite pup can look as camera ready as any of those dogs on TV. Take a look at your little guy: If your dog looks more like the canine equivalent of Julia Child than Julia Roberts, or more like Boy George than George Clooney, here are some show dog secrets unveiled.

Secret #1: Show Dogs Are Spotlessly Clean

Not all dog shows are held in glamorous arenas like Madison Square Garden. Most are held at county fairgrounds or local expo centers. However, no matter where the locale, the dogs are primped, bathed, and blow dried to perfection. Many shows are 3 or 4 days of consecutive

showing, and the dogs are bathed and groomed every day.

If you want your dog to look like the show dogs do, he needs to be spotlessly clean—no stringy hair, no mats, no smelly ears. Coat type doesn't matter—short coats can gleam just as much as long coats, and even the "naked" hairless dogs must be clean.

Turns out, the biggest beauty secrets of the show dogs is one you've already heard from your mom—cleanliness is beautiful.

Secret #2: Show Dogs are Faultlessly Groomed

If you go to a dog show, wander into the area where the handlers (or the full-time groomers they sometimes employ) are getting the dogs ready. A clean dog is just the start for these competitive canines. No matter what coat type, time is spent combing and brushing a show dog. And long-haired breeds might spend an hour

What does it take be a winner? Perfect grooming is a good start.

or more on the grooming table—every single hair carefully, painstakingly brushed, combed, and placed where they will look the best.

Your dog probably doesn't have any interest in spending an hour of his life getting combed, and that's okay. But do follow the show dog secret of combing out your dog regularly, making sure to comb down clear to the dog's skin. This way, he'll look and feel as fabulous as any champion.

Secret #3: Show Dogs Accept Grooming With Grace

Grooming is a major part of a show dog's life, and he must learn quickly to tolerate and even enjoy it if he's going to be a competitor. While your little dog might not need the intensive grooming of the show dog, he's still going to need to be groomed. If he's a long-haired dog, he needs daily brushing and combing. Even if he's a short-haired dog, he'll need frequent baths (after all, you want him sweet and clean-smelling in your arms), regular tooth brushing, nail trimming, and general maintenance. That's a lot of time having his little body poked and prodded.

If he sees grooming as torture, he's going to spend a lot of hours as an unhappy dog—and an unhappy dog is no fun to groom. It's your job to help your dog to think that grooming is a happy experience. How do you do this? By pairing grooming behaviors with happy, tail-wagging times with your pet.

Wraps keep the coats of these show dogs looking good.

Teach "Lift Up"

Grooming a small dog usually happens on your lap, in a sink, or on a table. This means that your dog has to be lifted into the air to be groomed. Much of the conflict with grooming little dogs stems from the fact that they might hate to be picked up! You can reduce your dog's stress (and your own) by teaching your pup the Lift Up command.

Think how scary it must be for your little dog to be lifted off the ground. Compared to your pint-sized pooch, you're about the size of a five-story building. From your dog's point of view, a huge hand comes flying out of the air, picks him up, and does strange things to him. Of course he doesn't like it.

You can teach him to tolerate it, and even like it, by letting him know what is going on. Every day, pick up your dog with a cue word such as "Lift Up" (or "Up, Up, Up," whatever feels natural for you to say). Be sure to hold his body comfortably, supporting his chest and rear; being picked up around the ribs or having his back legs dangling in the air can be extremely uncomfortable for your dog. When you've picked him up, tell him, "Good dog!" and give him a treat. Repeat this frequently, and soon he'll welcome being picked up.

Teach Your Dog the Names of His Body Parts

Imagine someone grabbing at parts of your body with no warning. You'd probably consider biting anyone who did that to you. You're able to accept being touched by your doctor, hairdresser, or massage therapist,

Is That Dog a Real Blonde?

Admittedly, rumors always surface some show dogs have a coat color enhanced from a bottle. While that generally isn't true, many of the dogs do have some "legal" help, like combing in white powder into a white dog's coat to make it bright and shiny. A little enhancement, such as a little dark makeup to make a nose a tad blacker is certainly not unheard of. Groomers will spray hairspray all over a big Poodle haircut, and then clean off every bit of hairspray when the show is over.

What's not true are rumors of facelifts and tummy tucks on show dogs. That's left to human starlets, thank goodness.

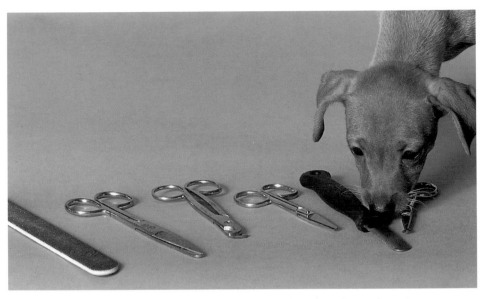

You'll find using high-quality grooming tools makes the job much easier.

because you know and expect to be touched. If you teach your dog the names of his body parts, he'll understand that those areas will be touched, and he'll be much calmer when he's being groomed. (It's also very helpful at the veterinarian's office).

Start out with a gentle touch, and a quick food reward. For example, touch his toes gently, say, "Good feet!" and give him a favorite treat. Use this reward-based method to teach him names for his eyes, ears, feet, nose, tail, teeth, tummy, and rear end.

As he's comfortable with his body parts being touched lightly, make the exam more probing, as it would be when he's being groomed or is at the veterinarian's. For example, after your dog calmly accepts having his feet touched lightly, begin to gently examine between the pads of his feet. After he's accepted having his muzzle touched, begin to look at his front teeth, and later his back teeth—always rewarding the behavior with yummy treats.

Over time, he'll associate being touched—even in delicate areas—with a happy experience. Always make this touching fun. It's a happy time between the two of you. Ask other people to touch your dog as well, and have them give your dog the treat.

A little white powder can hide those embarrassing blemishes.

Secret #4: Show Dogs Get the Best Products for Their Hair

Don't hate these dogs because they're beautiful—just use the same fabulous hair products! Go to most dog shows, and you can find vendors selling an amazing array of hair care products for all kinds of coats. From shampoos and conditioners to sprays and spritzers, each handler has a special concoction for each different dog. You can find all-natural, great smelling, extra-shine products—anything you can think of for human hair has probably been made for your little guy.

Secret #5: Show Groomers Have the Best Equipment

Groomers have totally cool equipment. It's not unusual for them to have a dozen different pairs of scissors, each with a specific purpose. Long, rounded shears shape Bichon 'dos. Thinning shears make the back of a Papillon's ankles look slender and sleek. While you don't need all that equipment, you should think about what you do need to keep your dog's coat looking trim and tidy. It's worth it to invest in well-made grooming tools, and then make sure you use them!

secret # 6: Show Dogs Know What to Wear

Show dogs just wear a tiny lead in the ring, but that leash is chosen with great care. The handler might choose a color that contrasts with the dog's fur (a purple leash might set off a fawn-colored dog) or choose a leash that emphasizes a great feature (such as a black leash that shows off the dog's beautiful, dark eyes). Some breeds, such as Maltese and Shih Tzu, are shown with ribbons in their hair. Every colored ribbon is selected and placed on the dog to show off his sparkling eyes to their best advantage.

Secret #7: Show Dogs Get a Lot of Exercise

When you go to a dog show, you probably see dogs sitting around in crates, and feel sorry for them. The truth is that most of them get a lot of exercise. Many even have a regimen of walking, jogging, or running. Some handlers have treadmills to make sure the dogs log in their miles.

Exercise makes us all look and feel better, and your little dog is no exception. Your Pomeranian probably doesn't need a treadmill, but a nice walk every day is ideal. Play is also a great way to work in some exercise—chasing a ball across the living room floor for 20 minutes a day is great exercise for your little guy.

Secret #8: Show Dogs Have Great Teeth

Show dogs have dazzling smiles that can rival the pearly whites of Tom Cruise or Faith Hill. How do these canine competitors keep their mouths in tip top shape? Their owners make sure to brush their teeth every day, because they that the build-up of bacteria in a dog's mouth can lead to kidney, liver, and heart problems.

Little dogs have worse dental problems than their larger cousins. Why? Little dogs have a full complement of teeth crowded into their little kewpie mouths. Also, a little problem that wouldn't mean much for a large breed can mean big trouble for a small one. A gum pocket of a millimeter isn't significant to a Labrador or a

Doggie Orthodontia

Yes, you can get braces for your dog's teeth. Certain veterinarians specialize in dentistry, and spend an additional 2 years of schooling learning the same skills as human oral surgeons and orthodontists. They do have appliances that can straighten a dog's teeth, but these are reserved for correcting a bite that's causing the dog a problem in eating, or making him physically uncomfortable. They don't fix that "snaggle tooth" unless there is a good reason for it.

If your dog's crooked smile doesn't get in the way of him eating and playing, you should learn to appreciate his slightly imperfect smile—think of it as adding character!

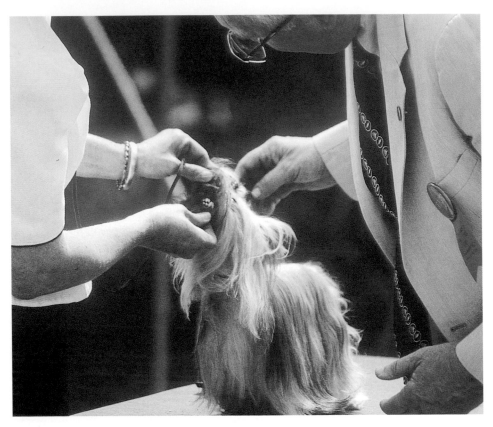

"Hmm. . . Perfect teeth <u>and</u> fresh breath—he's a winner!"

human, but it might be enough gum deterioration on a little dog to require a tooth extraction. The sad fact is that your small-sized dog is likely to lose a good number of those teeth during his lifetime.

It's even worse for the "smush-faced" breeds, such as Pugs, Pekingese, Japanese Chin, and Shih Tzu. Their flattened faces mean that their teeth don't align like they do on a regular muzzle, and that translates into more tartar build-up. Yikes.

Brushing Your Dog's Teeth

Your veterinarian can supply you with toothpaste formulated just for dogs. It comes in several flavors (most dogs prefer poultry-flavor!). This type of toothpaste has enzymes that will help break down plaque. Don't use human toothpaste—it will upset your pooch's tummy. Use the doggie toothpaste with a gauze pad, a small rubber brush that attaches to your finger, a cat toothbrush, or a child's toothbrush.

The key for tooth brushing is to gradually get the dog used to the idea. Here's how to work up to a full dental for your dog:

- ▣ Let him sniff the toothpaste and have a lick from the tube. Toothpaste formulated specially for dogs tastes great to dogs—let that be the reward. Plus, doggie toothpaste has enzymes that help break down tartar, so even licking toothpaste off your finger will help your dog's mouth get a little bit cleaner.

> ## Dental Floss Doesn't Work Without Opposable Thumbs
>
> I've had friends try to floss their dog's teeth. Trust me, that experiment isn't worth repeating. Instead, encourage your dog to chew on safe toys. Give him fuzzy toys to play with. Throw the toy, play tug of war, encourage him to squeak the squeaker inside. These toys can act much like dental floss to reduce the build-up of plaque. Also, you can try treats like Nutri-dents, which are safe bones that can help eliminate plaque build-up.

- ▣ Get your dog accustomed to having his head held and handled. A lot of the struggle of brushing dogs' teeth comes from dogs who are afraid to have their heads held still. So pet, hold, and cradle your dog's face. Give him treats, and tell him how great he is when you touch his face.
- ▣ Over time, acclimate him to having his mouth examined. Lift up his lip, take a quick look at a tooth, and reward him. When I look at my dogs' teeth, I say, "Teeth!" so they know I'll be poking around their mouths. Knowing what's coming next makes it less scary to your dog.
- ▣ Say "teeth" and gently insert your finger in his mouth, rubbing around his teeth. Reward your good little dog!
- ▣ Brush just one tooth, and tell your dog he's fab!
- ▣ Over time, brush additional teeth. Finally, work up to brushing his whole mouth (don't forget those hard-to-reach back molars).

While you brush his teeth, tell your dog he's gorgeous, and that you love his little pearly whites. When he's done, give him a smooch. After all, he won't have doggie breath if you keep up with the brushing!

"I'm ready for my close-up, Mr. DeMille!"

Secret #9: Show Dogs Are Told They Are Beautiful

Stand ringside at a dog show, and you'll see the handlers giving their dogs pep talks. Every handler truly believes her dog is the most beautiful in the class and deserves to win. Dogs are social animals who understand the intent of people in a very clear way. Watch the dogs move with grace, elegance, and joy. Why do they do this? Because they know they are great.

You don't need to be entered in a dog show to whisper to your dog that he's handsome, and that you think he's practically perfect. To you—he is!

The dogs on TV may be trying to win Best in Show, but your dog wins Best in Your Heart. Nothing is more beautiful than the dog who is sitting on your lap, sharing his soul with you.

Chapter 10

Pampering Your Pup:
Massages, Aromatherapy, & Other Remedies

Beauty is more than skin deep. This chapter is about feeling terrific in order to look terrific— especially if you have four paws and a tail.

Massage

When we think about a day at the spa, most likely we envision a relaxing, healing, life-affirming massage given to us by a skilled massage therapist. Well, your little dog can enjoy the benefits of a massage, too.

The Benefits of Massage

Aside from relaxation, massage has other benefits. Here are some of the reasons for your little dog (and you) to have a massage:

- ◎ Massage reduces anxiety and promotes a sense of well-being.
- ◎ Massage reduces fatigue.
- ◎ Massage promotes more rapid healing from injuries.
- ◎ Massage improves blood circulation.
- ◎ Massage stimulates the lymphatic system.
- ◎ Massage enhances the health and nourishment of skin.
- ◎ Massage can help manage chronic pain.

Finding a Trained Professional

More and more massage therapists are offering professional massage services for your dog. In fact, some massage therapists will treat both you and your dog in a visit together. (This just might be the perfect "spa" day with your dog!)

Most licensed massage therapists have completed at least a year of specialized schooling, and they have the training and knowledge to help an injured or sick animal. Some schools offer specialized courses for massage therapists to learn about animal anatomy and illnesses, giving them a wider range of skills. (One of those schools is the Northwest School of Animal Massage, which offers classes for both professionals and for people who want to learn more about massaging their own pets. Check them out at www.nwsam.com.)

Do It Yourself

While you'd want to go to a trained massage therapist to gain serious health benefits for your dog, an at-home massage can be bonding and relaxing.

To start, put on some favorite music and find a good place to relax. Have your dog in a position that's comfortable for both of you, whether that's on your lap, next to you on the couch, or maybe on the rug in front of the fireplace.

Gently stroke his fur, from above his eyes, over his head, down his back, and then down his tail. Important note: If he doesn't like the touching, stop what you are dong—don't push it. Check with his veterinarian for medical or behavioral reasons why he may not enjoy the touching: He could be in pain, or he could need some help with behavioral issues.

Assuming he's happy with your touch, gradually put a little more pressure on his muscles. When he leans into you, massage deeply—he's asking you to! If you can, try to massage both sides of his body evenly. Imagine how frustrated you

Relaxation is th[e] key to looking good.

Physical Therapy for Your Little Dog

Sometimes massage isn't enough. Older animals with arthritis, dogs who have been in car accidents, even animals who have had sports injuries all may need professional physical therapy. Happily, a new field of physical rehab for pets has emerged to meet that need.

Veterinary rehab clinics use many techniques to strengthen your dog's muscles and reduce pain. These include underwater treadmills (a special treadmill encased in a plastic compartment that fills with water; it allows your dog to run without having to put all his weight on his legs); regular treadmills; therapy whirlpools; pulsed-signal therapy (a kind of magnetic stimulation); therapy balls; stairs (teaching dogs to use their back legs); painless electrical stimulation; stretching exercises; and other techniques used in human physical therapy.

would feel if someone only massaged one of your arms or half of your back. When you're done, lightly stroke his fur again.

When you massage your dog, breathe deeply, slowly, and regularly. It will relax both of you, and allow you to be more in tune with your dog's needs. This isn't the time to be thinking about the pile of work at the office or the chores you need to do around the house. Just enjoy the sweetness of your dog, and the bond of trust and love the two of you share. It's good for both of you!

Tellington Touch

Tellington Touch (also called TTouch) was developed by Linda Tellington-Jones. It's a system of feather-like touch that relaxes and calms a dog, and it can help you establish a closer rapport with your pet. It gives your pet a sense of well-being, and may help him feel better if he's sick. Because TTouch is much less intrusive than massage, it's a terrific alternative for animals who are sick, injured, or shy.

My little shy Papillon, Goldie, was touch-averse. For years, I tried to get her to enjoy petting. She eventually learned to tolerate it, but not enjoy it. Then, I took an excellent TTouch seminar, and Goldie discovered the joys of TTouch. At age 14, Goldie still doesn't enjoy being massaged or stroked, but when it comes to TTouch, she puts her little paws on my lap, wags her tail, and smiles, asking for more!

Several books and videos are available on TTouch, many of which are carried at local libraries. Many TTouch certified practitioners also teach classes, so you can learn and practice TTouch your own dog. Linda Tellington-Jones' web site (www.tteam-ttouch.com) gives a listing of TTouch practitioners around the world and also has books on the subject for sale.

Practical Reasons to Pet Your Little Dog Every Day

Did you know that cancer is the leading cause of death among senior-aged dogs? A weekly inspection of every inch of your dog's skin can help you find lumps and bumps early. Check for moles, warts, and thickening in your dog's skin. Ask your veterinarian to examine anything that looks the least bit suspicious. An early diagnosis could save your dog's life!

And dangers to your little dog's skin lurk right outside your home. Little dog beauties have to worry about something no runway model does: weeds called foxtails that can bury into your dog's skin and cause life-threatening injuries.

Foxtails aren't the same as the fur you might find on a coat collar. They are tall, grassy weeds, with a seeds that look like a barbed fishing hook. Foxtail seeds can enter a dog through his feet, nose, ears, and other skin areas. These horrible seeds migrate in the body—they've even been found in dogs' lungs. Once inside your dog's body, a foxtail usually has to be surgically removed.

Avoid walking in any area you know has foxtails. If your dog has been in a tall, grassy area, thoroughly comb him, and check his paws and ears. If you see any kind of seed or burr, be sure to get it off your dog immediately. If you suspect a foxtail is under your dog's skin (he has a painful bump, or seems to have something in his nasal passages or ear) take him to your

It's important to touch and pet your little dog every day.

veterinarian immediately. The problem only gets worse with time.

Foxtails are just one of the reasons that touching your dog all over his body every day is a life-saving idea!

Aromatherapy

You know certain smells can make you happy and feel better when you're down: the smell of baking bread; lavender in your bathtub; pine from a Christmas tree in the house. Aromatherapy takes the power of scent a step further—it uses the essential oils from certain plants to help us relax, balance, rejuvenate, restore,

Caution Around Candles

Some people love to light aromatherapy candles to scent their house. Be extraordinarily cautious around candles. Dogs jump on things, and a candle could easily be knocked over. And if you've got a cat in the house, they often like to bat the candle flame with their paws.

and enhance our bodies, minds, and spirits. Pure essential oils are extracted from many parts of a plant including the flower, leaf, resin, bark, root, twig, seed, berry, rind, and rhizome. Aromatherapy advocates believe that the application of these scents strengthens the body's self-healing processes by indirectly stimulating the immune system.

Essential oils can be irritating to an animal's skin, so it's not always easy to find safe oils for your little dog. Happily, the company Good Dogma (www.gooddogma.com) has a line of pet-specific soaps and spritzers that use essential oils to help benefit your dog.

Common essential oils and their benefits include:

- ◉ **Bay:** hair tonic, stimulant, antiflaking, antiseptic
- ◉ **Bergamot:** deodorant, insect repellent, antidepressant
- ◉ **Clove:** deodorant, repellent, antioxidant, stimulant
- ◉ **Geranium:** repellent, deodorant, antidepressant, antiseptic
- ◉ **Grapefruit:** antiseptic, toner, uplifting, hair tonic
- ◉ **Lavender:** deodorant, insect repellent, cleansing, soothing
- ◉ **Lemongrass:** antiseptic, deodorant, insect repellent, antioxidant
- ◉ **Peru Balsam:** good for dry irritated skin, soothing aroma

◎ **Rose:** antidepressant, hydrating, soothing, tonic
◎ **Rosewood:** deodorant, cellular stimulant, antidepressant
◎ **Sweet Orange:** anti-inflammatory, antidepressant, sedative
◎ **Tangerine:** antiseptic, sedative, tonic, toner
◎ **Tea-tree:** nature's heal-all oil, great for all irritations
◎ **Vanilla:** soothing, calming, comfort fragrance

I must admit I was skeptical when I bought a citrus spritzer—I thought my dogs would turn up their little noses at the scented spray. I was surprised when my dogs wagged their tails as soon as they smelled the clear, fruity scent—they clearly liked it. I'm not a perfume kind of person, but I liked the natural, clean scent, too.

The Skin He's In

Do you know the largest organ in a mammal's body? Nope, it's not the heart or liver or kidneys. It's the skin.

Take care of your dog's skin by giving him top-quality food, and possibly adding omega-3 fatty acids as a supplement. Use high quality shampoos and conditioners, and make sure he has plenty of exercise.

Sunburn

If you have a short-haired or shaved little dog, he can get sunburned. Protect him by putting sun block on his nose and other areas where the skin is exposed. Human sun block works just fine for your little guy.

Major Itches

If your dog is scratching and biting his skin, a trip to the veterinarian is in order. There's a good chance he has a skin infection, a flea allergy, or an environmental allergy. Veterinary dermatologists are specialists in allergies. If your veterinarian can't fix the problem, or relies only on steroids to suppress the itch, ask for a referral. Your veterinarian may perform allergy testing and prescribe shots. She may put your dog on an elimination diet, to see if the culprit is ingredients such as wheat, corn, or even chicken in his food.

The bottom line: Treat your dog's skin, and the health issues that relate to it, with the same care you do your own.

Health Care Is Essential

Massage, aromatherapy, and other healing modalities are wonderful support for your little dog. But, as terrific as they are, they don't replace good medical care from your dog's veterinarian. Basic health care is just as important to your dog as it is to you.

The reality is that your little dog's veterinarian is the most significant person in his life (after you). Make sure your dog never skips his regular annual check-ups (twice a year if he's an oldster), and follow your veterinarian's advice. The bottom line: Find a great veterinarian and listen to him or her!

"Naked" Dogs

If you've got a "naked" dog, skin care is a big deal. Breeds like Chinese Crested dogs are hairless except for tufts of fur on their heads, feet, and tails; Xoloitzcuintle (also called Mexican Hairless Dogs) and American Hairless Terriers (related to Rat Terriers) are completely naked.

You'd think care for these dogs would be a snap. After all, there isn't any hair to comb. Right? Wrong. Because the animals have no protective fur, their skin may be very sensitive to sun, cold, and wind. Some of these dogs can get cracked, dry skin if the skin isn't kept well-oiled. Hairless dogs need to wear sun block even when they're playing in the yard for just a few minutes.

Skin care is especially important for "naked breeds," like the Chinese Crested.

One woman explained that her American Hairless Terrier was higher maintenance than her kids. While other dogs' fur sloughs off mud from the yard, it sticks to her dog's skin. "I wash this dog more often than I wash my children," she jokes.

Alternative Medicine

In the last decade, human medical science has acknowledged the value of many kinds of alternative care. They're even doing acupuncture at Harvard University medical school!

Veterinary medicine has followed suit, and acupuncture, chiropractic treatments, herbs, homeopathy, and other alternative treatments are increasingly available for your little friend. Often, a combination of Western and Eastern medicine helps more than either one alone; for example, acupuncture after surgery can reduce pain and might just help the healing process.

We'll discuss some of the most popular alternative therapies include the following sections.

Acupuncture

In acupuncture, hair-thin needles are gently inserted into the dog's skin. A skilled acupuncturist does not hurt a dog when he inserts the needles. Unlike hypodermic needles, which are designed to pierce tissue to deliver a shot, the thin acupuncture needles are designed to go between layers of skin. Acupuncture can help many conditions, including pain, allergies, and circulation.

The International Veterinary Acupuncture Society (http://www.ivas.org) provides training and certification for veterinarians. Their web site includes a listing of certified members. (You may also consider checking with a human acupuncturist in your area, if your state medical and veterinary laws allow acupuncturists to treat animals.)

Chiropractic Treatments

This treatment consists of trained chiropractors or veterinarians realigning your dog's skeletal system to help keep it in healthy, functioning order. This can be very helpful after sports injuries (to which little dogs are just as prone as big dogs!), accidents, and other events that put your pint-sized pooch's body out of alignment.

The American Veterinary Chiropractic Association (www.animalchiropractic.org) provides training and certification for chiropractors and veterinarians. They have a list of certified practitioners on their web site, which are split fairly evenly between the two professions. Members are in the United States, Canada, Europe, and Australia.

Chinese Herbs

Chinese herbal medicine has been practiced for thousands of years. Chinese herbs can help treat many illnesses and, in some cases, may prove to be more effective than Western medications. Be sure that you are working with a skilled veterinarian (or the person prescribing the herbs is working closely with your veterinarian), because some herbs can interact with some medications. Don't treat your dog with herbs that you discover on the Internet or a late night infomercial on TV. Herbs are just as powerful as other medicines, and using the wrong herb in the wrong situation can be a serious risk for your little dog.

The American Holistic Veterinary Association (www.ahvma.org) has a good discussion of alternative therapies, including Chinese herbs. The web site also has a listing of members by state.

Homeopathy

First developed in the early 1800s, this system of healing is based on the basic concept that "like cures like." The idea is that a tiny dose of a substance can cure someone when a larger dose would make their symptoms worse. Much like a vaccine teaches the body to have an immune response to a disease by introducing a debilitated virus, homeopathy is designed to help the body overcome an illness by introducing a small dose of a substance that also helps the body's system learn to counteract the problem.

The Academy of Veterinary Homeopathy (www.theavh.org) trains and certifies veterinary homeopaths, and lists practitioners on its web site.

You might want to explore some alternative therapies with your little dog.

Section 3

Fabulous Inside & Out (Of The House)

This section gives you some great ideas about beauty and comfort for you and your dog—inside and outside of your home. Discover how to decorate your home with your diminutive diva in mind, learn how to celebrate the holidays safely, and enjoy new ways to party with your pooch.

You also need to know how to step out with your little dog. One of the many joys of having a pint-sized companion is that your little guy is so portable. You can take him with you to a meeting, fly with him to Paris, or drive cross-country—but no matter where you go, you'll know how to do it in style.

Enjoy!

Chapter 11

Carriers: Because Your Little Dog Can't Call a Cab

For millennia, dogs have been beasts of burden. They've pulled us in sleds across the frozen Arctic. They've carried us in carts in Europe. Indigenous American people fashioned travois that allowed dogs to pull humans and supplies across the plains. Nowadays, for our little dogs, we carry them everywhere! You have to wonder if our little dogs know they've gotten the better end of the deal.

Your portable pooch wants to go wherever you go. For many little dogs, the ticket to joining you on your jaunts is a carrier. In the last few years, the range of choices for pet totes has become dizzying. You can choose from a simple carrier for less than $30 to a Louis Vuitton model that will set you back a cool $1,470. There are pink carriers, crocodile-style leather carriers, and carriers that look like they're holding gym shorts. Some models allow your dog's head to stick out, and others make it impossible to guess that a dog is inside.

Shopping for a carrier is a little bit like shopping for a purse. There are functional things to think about, and after that—it's all a matter of style.

The Right Bag for Your Dog

You buy a little purse when you're planning an elegant evening out—its small size is perfect for carrying ID, a bit of cash, and your lipstick. For daytime, you might have a huge, honking mountain of a bag to carry your BlackBerry, checkbook, keys, wallet, makeup bag, a book to read in quiet moments, and coupons for a dozen different stores. Different tasks need different purses, and the same is true for dog carriers. You need a different carrier for a 3-pound (1.4 kg) Yorkie than for a 15-pound (6.8 kg) Pug.

If it's at all possible, bring your dog with you when you look for carriers, so that you can determine how his weight feels in the bag. Is the bag comfortable for him? Is he lost in the bottom, or is he sticking out the top? Does he like it? You'll find your dog may prefer some bags over others. Just like some women love the feel of a kicky Kate Spade purse to hang on to, other women will gravitate towards the classic elegance of a leather Coach bag. Much of it depends on how it feels in your hand.

You don't buy a pair of shoes without walking around the shoe department in them; do the same for your carrier. Carry your dog around for a bit. Is the bag comfortable, or does it bang against your legs? Does the shoulder strap dig into your flesh? Does it feel natural and easy?

A carrier can be a major purchase, so take your time and shop for a bag that works for both you and your precious passenger.

There are many types of dog carriers to fit your little dog's style.

The Boy's Club

Years ago, little dogs were often thought of as the purview of women, and the "big" breeds the domain of men. These more enlightened times allow men to enjoy a Miniature Pinscher as much (or more) than a Doberman Pinscher; he can be just as devoted to a Pekingese as a Pointer; and he can watch football with a French Bulldog on his lap rather than a Pit Bull at his feet.

Carriers also have changed with the times. Plenty of attractive bags in plaids and leather wouldn't be out of place with a man in a business suit. And the original Sherpa carrier bag looks more like a gym bag than a handbag.

Men enjoy little dogs for all the same reasons that women do: their personalities, their appearance, their convenience, and their portability. So, grab a bag that's right for you and take your friend with you wherever you go!

Quality

To determine quality, take a look at the bag's construction.

- Does it have a nice, sturdy bottom that will make your dog feel secure?
- Is it soft inside, or are there protruding bits of plastic or hardware that could injure your dog?
- Does the bag have a nice, removable pad in the bottom that you can wash if necessary? Are the straps securely anchored to the bag? You don't want them to break when you're carrying your dog through the rush-hour crowd in a big city.

Style, Style, Style

If you shop around a bit, you'll find countless bags that are the right fit for you and your dog. After that, it's all about personal preferences and style. It's all out there, from pink girly-girl to serious plaid, and "sneak bags" that look like briefcases to carriers that clearly show the dog inside.

Have fun shopping!

Carries Don't Work If Your Dog Refuses to Ride

Okay, you've got the hip carrier that reflects you and your dog's sense of style, and it's the right size and shape for your dog. You're ready to go out and have fun. But it's all for nothing if your dog screeches, screams, shakes, or jumps from the carrier. He needs your help in learning that carriers are his ticket to fun and freedom.

Think about a carrier from a little dog's viewpoint. You grab him and stuff him into a tiny space. Since he's (maybe) 10 inches (25.4 cm) tall, you're carrying him around at a level that, from his point of view, is equivalent to sitting in a three-story building. This contraption sways and maybe bangs against walls. It must feel sort of like going up in the Space Shuttle, but with no preparation. What's to like?

Teach your dog that his carrier is a great place to be. Make the bag like a drive-in restaurant for dog treats. Toss a treat in the bag, and let him run into the carrier and eat the treat. After he enjoys that, place him gently in the carrier and give him treats. Make a fuss over him. Tell him how handsome he looks. Every time you place him in the carrier, give him a special word so that he knows what to expect. So, say, "Carrier!" and then gently place him in the bag and fuss and treat.

Take your time in acclimating your dog to the carrier. You want him to think this is a good thing. Don't zip up the carrier until he likes sitting in it unzipped. Once he's learned that a zipped carrier has treats, then walk around your house with him, again telling him just how cool and fun this is. Then give him more treats. Take him for car rides in his bag, ending up at fun destinations. like the park or his favorite pet store to buy a toy.

Spend some time acclimating him to his carrier now and you'll have a dog who leaps joyfully into his carrier for a lifetime.

Flying With Fido: Airline-Approved Carriers

It all started with a flight attendant who loved her little Lhasa Apso, Sherpa. In 1989, Gayle Martz wanted to bring Sherpa with her when she traveled. She designed a lightweight, carry-on bag that fit

Teach your dog to accept his carrier, and your portable pooch can travel anywhere with you.

Your little guy may love your gym bag, but it's not the best way to travel with him.

under an airline seat. Instead of braving the dangers and desolation of flying in the cargo hold, Sherpa was able to travel in the cabin with Ms. Martz. She formed a company to manufacture and sell the bags, naming it in honor of Sherpa, the dog who started it all.

A whole new way of life for small dogs was born with that innovation. Ms. Martz successfully lobbied the airlines to change their old policies and permit small animals to travel with their families in the cabin. By 1994, the Sherpa Bag had become the officially approved in-cabin, soft-sided pet carrier for 10 airlines.

Sherpa Products is still the industry leader (and all of us who fly with our dogs owe this company a debt of gratitude), but several other companies now have airline-approved bags to carry your dog across the country and, in some cases, even to other countries.

If You Plan to Fly with Your Dog

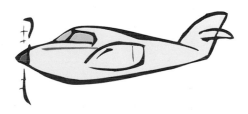

&. Make sure that you have a bag that is approved by the airline you will be flying. Not all tote bags for dogs are airline-approved. In fact, some companies (including Sherpa) make some products that are airline-approved and some that aren't. Don't arrive at the airport only to find that you don't have an approved carrier.

🐾 Pick the right carrier for your dog. The days are long gone when one size was supposed to fit all. The bags come in a variety of approved sizes and shapes. Purchase one that allows your dog to turn and lie down comfortably. It will make him happy, and it's required by the airlines.

🐾 Expect to pay for your pup's flight. Although you will be carrying your dog with you in lieu of a carry-on bag, airlines charge for this. The days are long gone when you might have been able to sneak a little dog on board (which was never a good idea anyway). With airport security systems now in place, you and your dog will be grounded if you haven't paid.

🐾 Make reservations well in advance. Airlines each have individual policies about how many dogs are allowed in the cabin. It can be as few as one or two for the entire plane. Make reservations early to make sure that your

You can modify a baby stroller to schlep your little dog.

dog has a place on the plane!

8. Train your dog to travel in his carrier. Acclimate your dog to his airline carrier, just as you would any other carrier. Drive him in the car in the carrier and carry him places in it. There will be enough new sights and sounds at the airport and on the plane—don't make the airline carrier a new experience, too.

8. Relax and enjoy the flight! Thousands of little dogs (and even some cats and a few other domestic animals) fly in cabins every day. Be grateful this is an option that's available to our little guys. It makes our lives and theirs so much better!

> ## What Not To Wear
>
> Be very aware of how your dog's body is being held in backpacks and other kinds of transportation. For a while, some popular backpacks sat a dog upright, much like a baby. That upright posture is normal for a human baby, but puts a significant strain on a dog's back. Select products that allow your dog to pick his own comfortable and natural position, whether it's sitting or lying down.

Other (Fashionable) Ways to Schlep Your Dog

You now know about the fashion carriers that are available for your little dog, and that's a great way to transport him guy most of the time. However, carriers have their limitations. You hold a carrier by a handle, or with a strap across your shoulders. This isn't the best way to carry an animal for very long distances or while you're vigorously exercising.

Alternatives to carriers are available that allow you to comfortably carry your little dog, including backpacks, slings, and carriages. It's a burden that we're happy to bear for our little guys.

Who Needs the Extra Help?

I have two younger dogs and one senior who is 14. Goldie, my senior, is just getting to the point where one of our long, vigorous walks is sometimes too much for her. So far, I've just scooped her up and carried all 6 pounds (2.7 kg) of her home in my arms. If she comes to a point where a walk is uncomfortable for her, or most of the walk is, I'll use an alternative, such as a

Your little dog might tire quickly, so think of fun ways to transport him.

backpack or carriage, to bring her along for the ride. The younger boys will still get their vigorous walks, I'll get my exercise, and Goldie will be there with the family.

Keep in mind that young puppies, older dogs, and dogs who may be recovering from an injury or an illness can tire quickly.

Then, some breeds just aren't built for speed or distance, but still love to be with you for your walks. For example, Pekingese or some Chins have a limited distance they can comfortably walk at any speed. Dogs like this can all be good candidates to ride for at least part of the walk

What To Try for Walks

For walks, a carrier might not be very comfortable for you or your dog, especially if you're covering long distances or trying to walk at an aerobic pace.

&. **Backpack-style Carriers.** These can be a terrific alternative for schlepping your little guy. Sherpa has a few models that are backpacks and also airline-approved carriers.

❧. **Dog Strollers.** These are modeled on baby carriages, but have enclosed areas in which your dog rides. Many models are on the market, of varying sizes, shapes, and design features. A great place to look is www.justpetstrollers.com. For a less fashionable, but more affordable option, check out baby resale shops for a used stroller, and create your own modifications to keep your dog in place while he rides.

What To Try for Vigorous Exercise

You may want to run 5 miles (8 km) a day, but your Shih Tzu doesn't. You might want to take your dog for a bike ride, but his tiny legs aren't going to keep up with you. Happily, solutions exist for jocks who love dogs who aren't.

If you're a jogger, check out the pet jogging stroller—designed like a baby jogging stroller, but made to keep your pet contained. One model, the AT3 All-Terrain Pet Stroller, includes features such as three-wheel design, a cup holder, a storage basket for your dog's toys and treats, and rear-wheel shock absorbers.

Bicyclists can purchase covered carts to pull behind your bike, available at major retailers such as Target.

When Not To Schlep

I was talking to a friend who teaches obedience classes lately, and she was worried about the puppy class that was about to start. A new customer had called to sign her Bulldog up for puppy kindergarten. In the preliminary chat, it came out that the puppy never went for walks—ever. The woman had bought the pup a carriage and pushed him everywhere.

With practice and the right equipment, your Yorkie might be the next Venus Williams.

Although there are many fabulous ways to schlep your dog, nothing can take the place of exercise.

Puppies and adult dogs, like kids, need exercise. They need to walk, run, jump, and play.

If a dog can't walk a normal distance for his breed and his age, discuss the issue with your veterinarian right away! He may need some orthopedic veterinary care. In some cases, early intervention makes all the difference in a good outcome.

So, use a carriage or backpack for a dog who needs an occasional boost or wants to come along on a vigorous activity. Don't let this useful tool deprive a normal dog of the routine exercise he needs to stay healthy.

Chapter 12

Road Trip!
Rules for Roaving With Rover

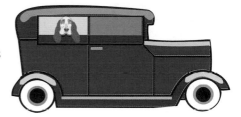

Crank up the radio, get out your favorite CDs, and fill up the gas tank. Any dog and human who look as good as the two of you need to have some fun on the road. Whether you and your pint-sized companion are traveling across country, or just across town to visit friends, go out and have a good time together.

Traveling Necessities

You don't drive without your seatbelt on, and most likely your car has airbags to keep you safe. You also worry about the safety of your human passengers—you would never, ever consider driving a block with a 10-pound (4.5 kg) baby loose in the front seat of a car. You know that if you were in a car accident with that baby, chances are that the child would end up with severe injuries. A lot of scary things happen to a small body in an accident: the force of the collision, flying into a windshield unrestrained, the explosion of the airbag. It's illegal to allow a baby to ride loose in the front seat of a car because it's so dangerous.

It's just as dangerous for your little dog. Your dog should ride in a crate in the back seat. The crate must be securely held in place with a seatbelt.

Even though your Yorkie would love to drive, he's better off in his crate when you're on the road.

Of course this doesn't seem as fun or joyful as riding with your little dog on your lap. But you will never forgive yourself if you're driving in your car and your little buddy dies because he wasn't in a safe place.

Large dogs may be safe enough with restraint from a doggie seat belt, but that's not enough for a little dog. A seatbelt doesn't protect the small dog from the explosion of an airbag. Always, always, always have your dog ride in his crate, tucked safely away from deploying airbags!

The crate for your car can be a sturdy plastic crate or a well-constructed wire one. I leave my dogs' crates in the car all the time, so I just pop them into their crates, and we're off on our road trip to have a great time.

Buy a crate today for you car, and always use it. If you ever have that fender-bender and the airbags deploy, you will be so grateful that your dog was someplace safe.

Other Safety Precautions

⚙ **Sunshine Kills.** Don't leave your dog in a parked car in the summer. Even if you park in the shade, the car can reach 120°F in minutes. Your dog's body

Are We Having Fun Yet?

Think ahead about whether your destination will be a fun place for a little dog. If you're going on a business trip, and your dog will be alone in a hotel room all day, maybe he'd rather stay home with friends or a professional pet sitter. If you're visiting your sister, her 18 rambunctious kids, and her 9 big dogs, maybe he'd rather be a no-show.
If your dog won't have fun, don't take him. You'll both be happier.

doesn't deal as well with heat as a human's can, and he could die while you make a quick stop at the grocery store.

🐾 **Lock Your Doors and Roll Up Your Windows.** It's easy for bad people to steal little dogs from a car. All it takes is for someone to reach in and grab your sweet guy. I met a woman whose small dog was stolen from her car when she went into the gas station to pay for gas. Never leave your dog alone in an unlocked car, and don't leave him alone with the windows opened a bit for safety—you may return to an empty car.

Packing for Your Prince or Princess

Break out the matching Louis Vuitton luggage and be sure to bring the following for your little darling:

🐾 Leash and collar
🐾 Water bowl
🐾 Food
🐾 Treats
🐾 Toys
🐾 Favorite blanket
🐾 Baggies (for clean-up)

If your dog doesn't travel often, or if he tends to get tummy upsets, bring along water from home or bottled water for him. Keep your dog's supplies in a separate bag, with the water bowl and baggies on top, where it's easy to reach them when you make "pit stops" for your dog.

Of course, if you have a well-dressed dog, he might have a second suitcase of appropriate clothing for your activities when you reach your destination.

You might want to skip the motorcycle in favor of a motorcycle jacket for your tiny pooch.

Kings of the Road: Planning Your Pooch-Friendly Trip

Gone are the days when dogs were only welcome in places that resembled the Bates Motel from the movie Psycho (complete with Norman waiting for you in the shower). Nowadays, especially if you have a little dog, your furry family member will be welcome in most places you'd want to stay. From economy-minded Motel 6 to the sumptuous Ritz Carlton on Central Park, more savvy businesses want you to stay with them than every before.

Dozens of web sites and books can help you plan a dog-friendly vacation, from places to stay to routes to drive. My favorite travel website is www.petswelcome.com. This site gives accurate, up-to-date information about over 25,000 pet-friendly hotels, ski resorts, bed and breakfasts, and campgrounds. The site even provides driving instructions to locations, showing

ID Your Dog

Any time you travel, be sure your pet has his ID tag on his collar. If you're on a long-distance trip, give him a second ID tag that includes the name and phone number of the person to contact at your destination.

pet-friendly lodging along the way. You can even ask for directions going along back roads rather than freeways, just to make your trip more fun.

Another great resource is AAA. Their members have learned to trust the organization's advice on all kinds of travel, and that includes the most recent edition of *Traveling with Your Pet: The AAA PetBook*. Go to www.AAA.com to find out more.

> ## Don't Sneak In
>
> A growing number of stores, hotels, and public places welcome small, well-behaved dogs. If your dog isn't welcome, take your business someplace where he is. Don't lie and sneak your dog in where he isn't allowed.

A lot of travel books about various regions of the country and big cities also are available. Some include hiking information, or rate local parks.

You and your dog have a wonderful relationship already. You enjoy going places together. Go have the adventure of a lifetime!

Petiquette: Rules for Roving With Rover

You love your dog, and in your eyes, he may do no wrong. But any time you travel with him or take him out, you must be aware of his behavior, and how it is affecting the lives of other people.

Here are just a few pup "petiquette" pointers for you to ponder.

Petiquette Begins With "P"

Or maybe I should say it begins with "pee." No one else should have to deal with your dog's urine. Some owners don't bother housetraining their little dogs, and they can be little peeing machines. Many small-breed males are notorious leg-lifters. Here are some rules that you should consider before you and your dog go out and about:

- Retailers can't sell merchandise after your dog pees on it. If your dog pees on anything in a store, you should buy it.
- If your dog has an accident in someone's home or business, tell them and then insist on cleaning it up.
- If you're not sure if your dog will mark, don't give him the chance to show you that

Whether you are traveling with your little dog, or just going for a walk, remember to observe proper rules of "petiquette."

he will. Hold him in your arms or in his carrier. Another alternative is to put a belly band on him—a device that will capture any urine.

While We're on the Subject...

Always, always, always pick up after your dog poops. You can stick little sandwich-style plastic baggies in your pockets and have one ready every time. No one wants to walk in a park or down a city sidewalk and step in your dog's poop.

It's totally unhip to pretend you don't notice what your dog is doing and then nonchalantly leave the evidence behind. You aren't fooling anyone!

It's Okay for Others to Just Say "No"

Of course, you have the most adorable, funniest, brightest dog in the history of the Western world. And yeah, people might feel better if they had a chance to know him better. But this is a free country, and people have the right to say "no" about having their personal space invaded. So, if someone asks you to hold your dog back, or if he doesn't want to pet or cuddle—that's okay. And, if someone says that your dog isn't playing nicely with another dog, just accept them at their word.

You know that 99 percent of the people and dogs love your little buddy, but the other1 percent has the right to be blind to your dog's charms.

It's Okay for You to Just Say "No"

Not every dog is a social butterfly. Some are shy when people or other dogs come too close, others might be aggressive. Some are a combination of the two.

If you feel that a person or animal is making your dog uncomfortable, don't make your dog suffer. Just say that your dog needs a little more room, or that he doesn't want to play right now. Then pick him up and take him away from the difficult situation. No rule says that you have to let every stranger touch your dog, or that your dog has to endure harassment from a small child or an adult who won't pet gently or respect your dog's space.

When you're out having fun with your pup, make sure others respect his space.

Unless you are sure a larger dog is well-socialized, you might want to stick with play groups just for small dogs.

You know, people buy big dogs for protection. Maybe your little dog picked you to be his protection! Don't let him down.

Cheating Isn't Pretty

Some unscrupulous people get their dogs into stores and restaurants by telling the business that the dog is a service dog. That's just plain wrong.

A service dog is trained to provide needed help to a person with a disability. Their jobs include the well-known tasks of working as a guide dog for a blind person or a hearing dog for a person who is deaf. More service dogs than ever before are being used for other kinds of assistance, such as picking up items on the floor, opening doors for a person in a wheelchair, or providing balance for a person with poor mobility. Many people with invisible disabilities have service dogs, such as dogs who alert their humans to the beginning of a seizure, heart problems, or dropping blood sugar levels. Just as a person with a disability has the right to go into a restaurant, grocery store, or airplane with a wheelchair or cane, they have the right to go into those places with their invaluable service dogs.

When people lie and say that their little companion is a "service dog," it makes it that much harder for service dogs to be allowed where they legally have the right to be. It's just as bad as parking in a handicapped parking space.

Personally, I think dogs should be welcome in stores, restaurants, and everywhere else I go. We haven't all died of some dog-borne disease now that service dogs come in these places. And French people are healthier than Americans, and dogs are allowed everywhere in France. I'm all for protesting the current rules and for refusing to do business with companies that don't welcome my four-footed family members. Just don't call your dog a service dog—that jeopardizes someone else's rights for your convenience and enjoyment. And that's not beautiful or stylish.

Dog Parks and Play Group Etiquette

Think twice, and then think again before taking your little dog to a dog park. Some sturdy, rowdy small dogs, such as Jack Russell Terriers or West Highland White Terriers admittedly usually do very well playing with big dogs. However, even a friendly big dog can seriously hurt a Chihuahua or Yorkie even in well-intended play. So, for most dogs under 20 pounds (9kg), and all dogs under 10 pounds (4.5 kg), dog parks aren't a good idea.

Play groups for same-sized dogs are a great alternative! Most dogs love playing with dogs that are about the same size. Still, play groups (much like ones for kids), require sharing and good manners. Not all dogs like playing in groups with strange dogs. Take your dog out of a situation if:

- 🐾 He bites or chases other dogs. It's no fun for dogs of any size to deal with a bully—and a dog that is mean to other dogs is a bully.
- 🐾 He's scared. If your dog is cowering in a corner, or if another dog is bullying him, don't keep him in misery. Whose idea of fun is that?

Chapter 13

Exercise, Sports, and Dressing Your Active Dog

It's time to talk about your little dog's fitness regimen. Our sports heroes are admired for their competitive spirit and buff bods. Participating in organized dog sports or finding something active to do with your little dog is a great way for both of you to stay healthy. Yes, your little dog can be a sporting dog.

Okay, technically, "sporting dogs" are breeds like Labrador Retrievers, German Shorthaired Pointers, or Springer Spaniels who were bred to hunt, retrieve, and swim in icy waters. Your little guy may be more of a sportswear dog.

Still, many small dogs have a lot more pep and energy per square inch than any Golden Retriever. While a Pekingese might find a jaunt across the living room tiring, all the small terrier breeds, and little guys including Papillons, Miniature Pinschers, and Chinese Crested Dogs, can thrive on long walks, hikes, and exercising with you.

Your small dog might not want to leap into a cold river to retrieve a duck, but chances are he'd love to go boating with you and cruise around your local lake. Your dog will enjoy the time spent living the sporting life with you, as long as you keep him well-equipped and safe.

Walking and Hiking

Walking is the best form of physical activity for both humans and their dogs. Not only is it physically healthy, it's emotionally healthy. Dogs bond in a special way during a walk—it seems to remind them of the joys of living in a great pack.

While walking is wonderful exercise, be aware of your little dog's fitness level. Every step you take may be a dozen or more on your dog's little feet. Watch him carefully for signs of tiring. Is he carrying his head or tail low? Is he stumbling? Is he lagging behind you? If so, you might want to pick him up and carry him.

Jogging

Most dogs under 20 pounds (9 kg) aren't good candidates as jogging partners. Even if they can somehow keep up with you, they certainly aren't having fun. There are some exceptions. Long-legged terriers like Parson Russell Terriers (the long-legged Jack Russells), oversized Papillons (taller than about 12 inches (30.5 cm) and lanky in build), and Miniature Poodles may sometimes be happy jogging companions, as long as the pace and distance is reasonable. Look at the build and stamina of your dog, and do what's right for him. If you're a jogger and your dog isn't, carry him in a backpack or push him in a stroller; you can spend the time together without asking him to do something that his body just can't do.

Important exercise note: *Even if you have a real doggie athlete, don't take him running until he is at least 12 to 18 months old, and only after your*

Sports gear can be fashionable and fun.

Good Thing She's a Little Dog!

My Papillon Goldie spent all of her time indoors, most of it in a crate, before she came to me when she was 2 years old. For the first few weeks I had Goldie, we took walks in the city neighborhood I was living in at the time. At the end of the day, you could see the girl stretching her tired muscles—obviously the fitness regimen was taking some getting used to for her.

I'm a pretty active person, and I decided one weekend that Goldie would enjoy a hike in the forest. On a beautiful autumn day, we went to a state park to take a leisurely hike along a trail that rises a couple of miles in an area of beautiful waterfalls. It was about a 5-mile (8 km) hike. Goldie was fine the first 3 miles (4.8 km) or so. Then, she looked at me, sat down, and made it clear she would go no farther.

I felt so guilty—I'd asked her to do more than she could do. I was lucky I had a dog who had the kind of personality to tell me when I'd made a mistake. Some dogs would have kept walking until they were ill. I was grateful that Goldie told me what she needed. I was also grateful I had a 6-pound (2.7 kg) dog—not a 60-pound (27.2 kg) one—as I carried her down the return route of the trail.

It was a mistake I hope never to repeat with any dog. Even though Goldie was fine, that hike could have ended up hurting her. I built up her stamina slowly after that day and, over time, she became a fit and active little dog. At age 14, she still loves long walks.

Since that day, I have always watched her (and my other dogs) carefully during our walks. Now that Goldie is getting older, there are times when she likes a "ride" home in my arms rather than finishing the whole distance that my younger two dogs enjoy.

The moral of this story? Watch your dog carefully to make sure he's doing okay with the distance you're hiking, and be glad you happened to fall in love with a little dog on those days when you might need to carry him home.

veterinarian has given the okay! Dogs have growth plates in their bones that don't close until they are between about 12 and 18 months old. If you ask too much of your pup before he's finished developing, it could cause serious problems later in his life. Even if he's zooming around the yard, don't be tempted to ask him to jog with you. There is a huge difference between a pup running and resting at his own pace, and him trying to please you (and he may keep trying even after it hurts).

Boating with your little dog can be fun—just make sure he wears a safety jacket.

Send for My Yacht! Boating with Your Little Dog

Little dogs can make great boating companions. They're portable and they usually like the fun and excitement of being on the water. It's a great way to share the day with your dog as long as you put his safety first. Keep the following safety tips in mind:

❀ He should always wear a life jacket. Even if your dog is an excellent swimmer, he should always wear a jacket while he's in a boat. If your boat turns over, or if he slips overboard and hits his head, it doesn't matter how well he can swim. Be sure to select a good-quality life jacket that's well-designed for flotation. One good brand is the Ruff Wear Float Coat II, available at www.ruffwear.com. The sizes go down to extra-extra small.

❀ Watch for heat exhaustion. Keep your little guy cool and well-hydrated on sunny days. Remember, his fur won't benefit much from a cool breeze.

❀ Don't put him in a situation in which you wouldn't put a small child. Jet skis, goofy pranks on the water—not every shipboard moment is fun for a dog. Don't put your little one in harm's way. Better for him to stay home than to be hurt out on the lake or river.

Swimming Pools, Movie Stars...

Swimming pools are great luxuries to have, especially in warm climates. However, they can be a real danger to dogs, just as they can be to kids. Sadly, dogs have drowned in pools. It can happen to any dog.

Fence your pool securely, so that your pet can't gain access to the pool without you. It's best if you have a

Booties and Dog Backpacks

If you're hiking, you should consider booties for your dog. They're a good idea in urban neighborhoods, too, where asphalt can wear on paws and pavement can get hot in summer. Big dogs do great carrying backpacks, but it's not a great idea for a pint-sized companion. A dog shouldn't carry more than 10 percent of his weight in a backpack; what would be the point of having your little guy carrying 8 ounces?Just let him have a good time!

A relaxing dip in the pool is fine as long as you supervise your little dog.

Running Naked

If your dog got to choose what sport he'd like best, he might choose agility. This is an obstacle course for dogs, where they fly over hurdles, carom through above-ground tunnels, scramble up A-frames, and generally have as much fun as a dog can have with his fur on. It's also one of the trendiest sports in the dog world—its popularity has grown by leaps and bounds in the last few years.

Agility competition is divided by height, so little dogs have the same chance to win titles as they big guys. To learn more about this great sport, check out www.akc.org and click on "events." If you have a mixed breed, don't worry—there are organizations that welcome your dog in competition. Check out the North American Dog Agility Council at www.nadac.com and the United State Dog Agility Association at www.usdaa.com—both of these organizations welcome mixes and purebreds.

pool cover, so that the little guy can't fall in.

A device that can give you some peace of mind is the Safety Turtle alarm. This alarm is in the shape of a turtle, and is small enough to attach comfortably to a small dog's collar. If your dog falls into the pool, the alarm will sound.

Also, as a precaution, teach your dog where the swimming pool steps are, and how to use them. Mark the steps with a flag or other noticeable marker that is at your dog's eye level. Practice calling him to the steps and rewarding him with a delicious treat when he gets himself out of the pool. This could save his life!

Sports and Safety: Dealing with the Heat

Humans cool their bodies by sweating. Dogs cool their bodies by panting. However, the panting mechanism doesn't work very well on flat-faced breeds, including Pugs, Pekingese, Boston Terriers, French Bulldogs, Shih Tzu, Japanese Chin, and Brussels Griffons. These dogs can overheat and even die in conditions that wouldn't be a problem for most other breeds. You must be extra vigilant about watching your flat-faced dog in the heat! Senior-aged and overweight dogs also are at more risk than younger, more svelte, pointy-faced dogs.

Heat Exhaustion and Heat Stroke

Always watch for signs of overheating in your dog. While flat-faced breeds are at special risk, it can be a problem for any breed.

Here's what to look for:

Heat Exhaustion: Symptoms of heat exhaustion may include rapid panting, dry gums, muscle twitching, and extreme lethargy. If you hear a dry, raspy pant, stop the activity now and cool down your dog before the situation becomes serious!

Don't Forget the Sunscreen!

Dogs can get sunburned, especially on their noses and ear tips. Veterinarians say that dogs with light-colored noses or light-colored fur on their ears are particularly vulnerable to sunburn and skin cancer. Use sunscreen on your pooch when he's participating in outdoor activities.

Your little dog may excel in the trendy sport of agility.

Your cool little dog will need to cool down after he's had some fun in the sun.

Heat Stroke: Symptoms are heavy panting, glazed eyes, a rapid pulse, unsteadiness, a staggering gait, vomiting, or a deep red or purple tongue.

If you notice any of the above signs, here's what you can do:

- Cool your dog off! Use cool water (not ice water) and make sure it gets down to his skin, not just dripping off his coat.
- Cool him down by wrapping him in a towel soaked with cool water, placing him in a bathtub with cool water, pouring cool water over him (be sure to get the water onto his skin, not just his fur). You can also put ice packs on his head.
- Call your veterinarian (or an emergency veterinary clinic). Heat stroke is a complicated process that can involve organ failure; your dog can be dying even if he seems to be okay at first. Better to make an unnecessary call to your veterinarian than not to make a necessary one!

Chapter 14

Doing Home Décor
With Your Dog in Mind

Of course you have a great fashion sense. Take a look at your dog—no one could have such a cool little dog without a fabulous sense style. Just like interior decorators use an "inspiration piece" for the focus of their design, you can use your little dog to inspire your home decorating—in more ways than one.

Practical Inspiration

Hairs, spills, and accidents are a reality for those of us who have four-footed family members. Sometimes, practicality is the only inspiration you need.

Here are a few dog issues to think about when you're making choices in your home décor:

☒ Even if you have a white dog, white carpet is a really dumb idea. After all, your dog doesn't track in white mud. And, we won't even discuss the indignities to a carpet when your pup has eaten something indigestible. If you hate the idea of brown carpet (and most of us do), don't despair. Look for multicolored carpet with unpredictable patterns of color. Then, whatever stains end up in the carpet, it will look like it's part of the design.

- ☒ Carpet and pets can be a bad combination. Consider wood or hard-surface flooring. It's attractive and easy to clean up. Keep your dog's nails well-trimmed if you have hard-surface floors, so that he doesn't slip.

- ☒ Forget the horror stories about people who give away their dogs because the fur doesn't match the new couch. Be the kind of person who buys a new couch to match your dog!

- ☒ Okay, if you don't want to buy a new couch, consider slipcovers. They're trendy, come in a great array of patterns and materials, and are practical for dog-lovers.

- ☒ Even an afghan (the blanket, not the dog) thrown over the couch or bed can take a lot of stress out of the day. If your dog hops up on the afghan with his slimy leather chew toy, the couch is protected, and it won't raise your blood pressure.

- ☒ Look for dog beds and accessories that match your décor. If you like modern, you can find black, sleek dog beds. If you prefer traditional, you can find a nice denim bed that's easy to clean. Shabby chic more your style? A bed with lovely English rose design might work. Perhaps over-the-top glam is for you? In that case, you can find heart beds made of satin for your little diva. The choices are endless!

Dogs as Art

At the William Secord Gallery in New York, you'll see antique dog paintings for sale, some commanding six-figure prices. (See this magical place on the web at www.dogpainting.com.) From English manors to American historical homes, for years, great homes featured dog art on the walls. So don't be afraid to incorporate dog art into your own home.

You can find dog collectibles for every breed on eBay. Check out dog shows for more dog collectibles, from attractive stamps to old prints to pillows and throws in every breed. Collectible china plates and fine porcelain statues of your favorite breed are available, both new and vintage.

Check out the back of your favorite dog magazine, and you'll see plenty of ads for a professional photo session for your pooch. From beautiful black-and-white modern shots to traditional portraits, you can find a photographer to capture the quintessence of your little dog. Or, if you want to spend a little extra, you can have a portrait painted of your Mona Lisa in training. Either way, you'll have beautiful art for your wall, and a memory of your favorite little dog for a lifetime.

> ### Dish Tip
> Be careful when buying hand-crafted or imported food and water dishes. Be sure they're properly glazed so they don't harbor bacteria and make your dog sick. If you are using plastic dishes. they should be discarded if they develop scratches, another place where germs can hide.

Just do remember that, while it's fun to include your dog as part of your home décor, you don't want your house to end up looking like a kitschy kennel. As one of my friends put it, "Not every single thing that has a picture of your breed on it is attractive." Besides, your own little dog is a living piece of art to enjoy in your home every day.

Kitchen Kitsch

When we entertain, most of our guests find their way to the kitchen. It's only right that most dogs enjoy their food and water in the kitchen, too. Luckily for the style mavens out there, long gone are the days when a dog bowl had to be ugly. Artsy, humorous, even sophisticated—food and water dishes can add to the look of your kitchen. And the treat jar on the counter can be just as stylish as your espresso machine ever was.

There are plenty of ways to decorate your home using your very own beloved breed—just try and leave room for photos of your human family!

Every Princess (and Prince!) Needs a Bed

No dog-loving home is complete without a place for your little guy to sleep. Dogs, like humans, spend about a third of their lives asleep. Good sleep, for dogs and humans, is part of good health. It's the time our bodies repair the damage the day has done. It's when our immune systems kick back into place. It's when we dream.

Your little guy needs a safe, secure, comfortable place to rest—for his health and happiness.

Dogs in the Bed

Most small dogs sleep in bed with their human family.

Some training books say that is a bad idea, but in my opinion, in most cases it works out just fine. If you and your little guy are both comfortable, and he's not growling, snapping, or behaving badly in bed, just enjoy your sleep time together.

However, sleeping in bed isn't always what's best for the humans or the dogs. Don't feel guilty if you decide that

What pretty princess could resist such a bed?

your dog needs to sleep in a bed of his own. He'll be perfectly fine! If he's not in your bed, the best solution is a dog crate.

Comfy Crates for a Good Night's Sleep

Don't think of your dog's crate as a doggie prison. It isn't. A crate is a practical solution to bedtime woes, and I promise it will make your dog happy. Here's why a crate can be great!

Canine Contentment

Your dog sees a crate as his own little cave, his personal sanctuary space. Remember when you moved into your first little apartment and were so thrilled with the space? Your dog sees a comfy crate the same way. Think of his crate as his first compartment! In his crate, he doesn't have to worry about what's going on in the whole house; he can relax knowing that life is good in his crate.

Doggie Dreams

Dogs dream. You can observe your dog in his sleep, sometimes wagging his tail, barking, or growling. Some adult dogs make suckling sounds in their sleep, seemingly bringing back memories of their puppyhoods with their moms. Interestingly, studies indicate that small dogs spend more time dreaming than larger dogs. No one knows why. Don't you wonder what Freud would have to say about a dog's dreams?

Canine Confinement

Enclosing your dog in his crate for the night gives both of your peace of mind. You don't have to wonder if he's going to get up in the middle of the night and pee. He'll wake you up and tell you.

Confining your little guy in his crate also means he won't be getting up and moving from place-to-place during the night, so you'll get a good night's sleep, too. That will give you the chance to wake up fresh and invigorated—all the better to have fun with your dog the next morning!

Canine Comfort

Make your little buddy's crate a comfortable den. Put soft bedding in the bottom. As long as he's not a big chewer who swallows toy parts, put in a favorite toy at bedtime for him to snuggle with. He'll be every bit as happy in his bed as you are in yours.

Placing the Crate

Keep your dog's crate in the bedroom with you, especially if you have only one dog. While your dog certainly doesn't need to sleep on your bed, remember your dog is a pack animal. He'll feel most comfortable and secure when he's surrounded by his human pack. If you put his crate in the kitchen or basement, he'll feel banished and probably insecure. If you have two or more dogs, and they sleep in a separate room, that can work well, since your dog still has a pack to hang out with as he snoozes.

Acclimating Your Pooch to a Crate

If you have a new dog or puppy, or if you've decided that the dog who has been sleeping in your bed should be sleeping in a crate at least part of the time, it's easy to show him that sleeping in a crate is great.

Here's what to do:

 Select an appropriate crate. This crate is for sleeping, not for living in. Select a crate that is tall enough for your dog to stand, circle, and stretch out comfortably. Don't get a crate that is so large that he'll be tempted to play in it or pee in one corner.

 Make the crate cozy. Unless he's a chewer, line it with soft bedding. Put a toy in the crate. Make it a nice little sanctuary.

 When you bring the crate home, feed him treats in it. You need to be happy and positive, and show your dog this little compartment is a happy, positive place.

 Be sure he's gone potty before bedtime, so he has no reason to feel uncomfortable.

 Most dogs will enjoy their crates from the beginning. If your little dog is accustomed to sleeping in your bed and this is a change for him, he may whine or whimper a bit. Ignore him, and he'll find whining didn't work, and he will relax and go to sleep. As long as your dog is in the same room with you, he has no reason to feel insecure or afraid.

Ugly Crates and Attractive Solutions

I will admit it: Crates are ugly. They're made of either wire (which does look like prison, even though it isn't) or plastic. It's reasonable to think that the crate will clash with the décor of your home.

Here are some solutions that will make the crate much more attractive.

☑ Purchase a rattan-style crate. A few brands are available, but the most popular is the Bay Isle collection from Midwest Crates. These wire crates are woven with a nonabsorbent polyethylene material that looks like rattan. These crates are much more attractive than a typical dog crate, and they work fine for dogs that aren't chewers. (Big-time chewers will be too tempted by the rattan-type material.)

☑ Purchase a postmodern crate. If you're into sleek, postmodern décor, Bow Haus (www.bowhaus.ca) has designed a round, metal crate with side perforations; they say the crate can also be used as a side table.

☑ Use a crate cover. You can purchase fabric covers for your wire or plastic crate that softens the look. A small, lightweight crate like the Nylabone Fold-Away Den & Carrier would look smashing with a trendy leopard print cover. Or, you can also easily sew a crate cover yourself, choosing fabric that matches your bedroom décor.

Beds, Dog Sofas, and Chaise Lounges

If you want to save your couch, you might try getting your diva her own to lie on.

Go to any pet supply store or pet boutique, and you'll be overwhelmed by the choice of dog beds. You can find pink

Multiple-Dog Homes Need Plenty of Primo Spaces

If you have a multiple-dog household, it is important that plenty of comfy, desirable, cozy spots are available. You don't want two (or three or four) dogs arguing over who gets to stretch out on the couch. I have three dogs, and I have five comfy dog beds in my writing room, four in my living room (plus the people furniture), and even an extra one in my bedroom, in case a dog decides during the night that he doesn't want to share bed space with the other two.

Dogs, like kids, can have sibling rivalry. By providing multiple comfy spots around the room, each dog can find a comfortable place to relax, at a little distance from the canine "sibling" who is bugging him at the moment.

beds for princesses and four-posters for queens. Or buy a heart-shaped bed, like honeymoon resorts used to have. There are sofas, chaise lounges, and bean bag chairs.

The reality is that small dogs are generally comfortable anywhere. Dogs who are welcome on the human couch don't usually opt for a canine "bark-o-lounger." So, buy what appeals to you because it looks good to your eye, but don't be surprised when your dog opts to share your favorite chair instead.

"Arfs" and Crafts

The creativity that your dog inspires doesn't have to be limited to your décor. You can find your inner domestic diva for the doggie set. You can have parties and organize events that make the world a better place for animals—and for people, too. Creativity has never been more in style!

It feels good to make things for you friends, your dog, and yourself. Try a few of these ideas on for size:

- ☒ Create a web site for your dog. Keep a dog blog and report on his

Use your own creativity to make and decorate items for your little dog.

day! People from around the world who share your love of dogs will be able to "meet" him over the Internet.

☒ While you're on the computer, make your own greeting cards, holiday cards, and calendars using digital photos of your dog! Go to any office supply store, and you can get computer programs that turn your digital pictures into practical items. Next Christmas, let your favorite photo of your little Affenpinscher in his angel costume be the cover of your holiday card.

☒ If you want to make thoughtful gifts for friends, you can take photos of their dogs and turn them into calendars, cards, and posters.

☒ Scrapbooking has become a major American pastime. Craft stores are full of beautiful papers and products that will help you make a lasting record of the important people and places in your life. Remember, dogs are family, too. Give your dog his own scrap book (or several). You'll be able to keep track of his puppyhood and record his achievements, your good times together, and all the fun you've shared. When he's an old gray dog, you'll be so happy you have a book that brings back all those years of happy memories.

☒ Remember decoupage? That's the art form in which you use a special kind of glue to decorate objects with paper. Decoupage a toy box with pictures of fun chew toys ripped from magazines and keep your little guy's toys stored there. Or, you can find cigar box-shaped wooden purses at craft stores, and decoupage your little guy's mug to it, making a designer dog-loving original! Decoupage a treat canister with images of bones and give it, filled with yummie treats, as a gift to a dog-loving

A thoughtful handmade gift is always a great idea.

friend. It's a surprisingly absorbing and inexpensive hobby. And, if you take your time and use care with the technique, you can make some beautiful objects.

☑ Take a painting or drawing class—and use your dog as a model.

☑ Check out the ideas in the chapters on sweaters and collars for making your own beautiful creations!

☑ Creativity is cool, so have fun and find projects that you enjoy and can afford.

☑ Every dog is a muse under the fur.

Thoughtful Gifts

Sometimes, creativity is just coming up with the perfect gift for someone you care about. Here are a few ideas that might make someone's day a little happier:

☑ If you have a friend who has everything, don't hesitate to buy gifts for her dog. Pretty leashes, nifty beds, attractive sweaters, even those adorable bunny pajamas can be fun gifts for the friend who is hard to buy for. And, you don't have to worry about offending her if you buy the wrong size!

☑ If you have a friend who's fighting breast cancer, buy a pink ribbon collar for her dog and yours, showing your support for the cause. Coastal Pet Products sells collars and leashes with a pink ribbon design, and a portion of all profits go to the Susan G. Komen Breast Cancer Research Foundation. Planet Dog makes pink ribbon toys to support the Susan G. Komen Foundation, and blue ribbon toys to support the fight against prostate cancer.

☑ If you're bringing an ill friend some food or supplies, don't forget dog food and dog supplies. Offer to take her dog for a play date with yours, or to a spa session at your groomers. Friends help friends—and their dogs.

☑ Does your new friend have a puppy? Hold a puppy shower, so that all your human and dog pals can give the new pup toys, carriers, leashes, and sweaters.

☑ Don't forget the older dogs. When my Goldie turned 14, a friend made her a beautiful cake. (The cake was made of a bland meatloaf recipe, covered with pink icing made of cream cheese and oil, colored with food coloring.) It meant a lot to me to have this big milestone in Goldie's life celebrated!

☑ Make a donation to an animal charity in honor of your friend and her dog.

Creativity comes from the heart—the most important thing is to have fun with your little dog, and appreciate all the fun and joy he brings into your life. Stay stylish!

Chapter 15

Happy Howl-idays and Other Celebrations

Your dog is an important member of your family. Whether it's just the two of you, or you have some combination of two-footed and four-footed family members, more than likely, you'll want to include him in the celebration!

Obviously, many holidays have a serious religious significance and, chances are, the dog isn't part of that aspect of your holiday. However, all holidays also have their secular side. They're about gifts or costumes, family, and celebration. Why not let your "furkid" with the wet nose and wagging tail add to the joy of every holiday season? Just remember: While every holiday has its lighter side, it also has its own dangers. While you plan ways to celebrate the holidays seasons with your dog, also think about ways to keep him safe.

Here are a year's worth of holidays, from your little dog's perspective!

Easter

Something about the sight of bunny ears on a little dog charms even the most dour soul. Put a Chihuahua or a Yorkie in pink bunny pajamas, and you just want to coo until you're out of breath.

The Fun

Here are some great ways to have fun with your little dog at Easter:

Easter Egg Hunts

Dogs love hard-boiled eggs. Put colored eggs out and let him go on his own Easter egg hunt. Better yet, team him up with a gentle child—the two of them will be the winners in any contest to find the most eggs! Reward the little guy for finding eggs by peeling one and feeding it to him, or, if he's very tiny, a bite of one. (Of course, check with your veterinarian before giving your dog an egg, especially if he has any tummy problems, allergies, or is on a special diet.)

Make Your Dog His Own Easter Basket

What could be happier than helping your dog find his own Easter basket? Fill it with dog cookies and treats, topped with an Easter bunny that squeaks. You can eat the ears off your chocolate bunny while your pooch chews the ears off his fuzzy one.

Spring isn't spring without a visit from the Easter Poodle.

The Dangers

Here are some things to watch out for when celebrating Easter:

Chocolate

Think of Easter celebrations, and you think chocolate. This is a serious danger to dogs—especially little ones. Keep chocolate out of reach of your little guy!

Easter Grass

Beware of that plastic Easter grass that comes in kids' Easter baskets. It may smell like candy to your dog, and he might decide to eat it. It's completely indigestible and, if it becomes lodged in his digestive system, it could require emergency surgery to remove it.

Rich "People" Food

Like all holiday celebrations that can include a big meal, make sure no one is feeding your little guy table scraps. Pancreatitis can develop when dogs eat foods that are too rich—and the condition can be deadly. Remember, tiny dogs eat tiny bites. Wolfing down those big pieces of rich meats or gravies can really endanger your dog's life.

Spring Clothes

Easter is the time when we bring spring clothes out of the closet. Make sure that little sundress still fits your girl. If not, maybe you should talk to your veterinarian about developing a sensible diet and exercise program that will help her take off those winter ounces!

The Fourth of July

Frankly, for dogs, the Fourth of July isn't a lot of fun. The bursts and booms of fireworks are terrifying to many dogs. The Fourth of July is the number one holiday for dogs ending up at shelters and emergency clinics.

Have fun this holiday season by staying home with your little dog, or going to someplace quiet in the country. This may sound unpatriotic, but maybe this is a good week to take your dog with you on that dream vacation to France, Canada, or England, where July 4 is just a quiet day on the calendar.

Of course, you can show your patriotism (and your dog's) by dressing your little guy in a red, white, and blue bandana. It's a nice way to express your love of country, without the frightening noise. For most dogs, Independence Day comes on July 5, when things get quieter and the world feels safer again.

The Dangers

While most people like the excitement of unexpected noises, dogs and other animals are hard-wired to run at the sound of fireworks. Every year, thousands upon thousands of four-legged family members escape from their homes—running in panic. Don't let your dog become a statistic at an animal shelter—or worse yet, at an emergency clinic.

Here are some tips that can help prevent tragedy.

Don't Take Your Dog to a Fireworks Celebration

He may panic and leap from your arms in the middle of a huge crowd. Even if he doesn't panic, the noise isn't fun for him. The bottom line: Even if you have an easy-going, happy-go-lucky dog, leave him safely at home rather than take a chance that he'll be miserable at a fireworks display.

Keep Your Dog Indoors

A backyard that's safe and secure for some playtime 364 days a year might not be enough to contain your dog when fireworks start. Dogs who are usually perfectly content playing in the yard will jump,

Fireworks aren't fun for your dog—keep him inside for the Fourth of July.

When the Terrors of the Fourth of July Last All Year Long

For many dogs, the fears that come on the Fourth of July are an everyday event. For dogs who worry year-round, it's important to get professional help. Ask your veterinarian to refer you to a veterinary behaviorist. These trained professionals are basically the psychiatrists of the dog world.

A veterinary behaviorist can work with you to develop a treatment plan for your dog. The plan should include identifying things that trigger a dog's fear and counter-conditioning the dog—teaching the dog to replace a fearful response with a relaxed one. For example, you may play tapes of thunderstorms at a very soft volume, while your dog gets treats and playtime. Over time, the tapes are played louder and louder. For many dogs, a program of gradual desensitization helps them learn to stay calm. In more difficult cases, the dogs may also receive prescription medication in addition to behavior modification.

climb, or claw their way over the fence. Yes, even your little dog will do unimaginable feats to get away from the noise that terrifies him.

Your dog should be inside before the noise of July 4 starts (this also hold true for thunderstorms, which many dogs are afraid of). Close the drapes, and put on "white noise" such as background music—something with a strong bass beat that diffuses the noise of the day.

Try Nonprescription Calming Formulas

If you have a dog that you know is sensitive to sound, try some remedies that fall under the category of "might help, can't hurt."

One clinically proven calmer is called Comfort Zone with DAP. DAP is an acronym for "Dog Appeasing Pheromone." This product mimics the smells that a female dog generates to give her puppies a sense of well-being, according to the manufacturer, Farnam Pet Products. DAP reduced stress-related behaviors such as excessive whining and barking as much as 85 percent in clinical trials. It's odor-free to human noses, and doesn't have any side-effects, so it's worth trying. Ideally, you should start using the product at least 2 weeks before you expect trigger events for your dog's anxiety. You can purchase it at veterinary offices; the product comes in a diffuser that lasts for a month.

You also might want to try Rescue Remedy, a distilled flower essence available at health food stores. This is a calming, homeopathic formula that seems to help some dogs (and people) and also has no side effects.

Halloween

Dogs love tricks. Dogs love treats. So this holiday can keep their tails wagging!

The Fun

Here are some great ways to have fun with your little dog this Halloween.

Costumes!

If your dog is accustomed to wearing coats, sweaters, and even dresses or sunglasses during the rest of the year, you are going to have a blast dressing your "furkid" up for Halloween.

Countless costumes are for sale at pet supply stores, pet boutiques, Internet pet sites, and even grocery and department stores. Fairy princess or wicked witch, cheerleader or Superdog, cowboy or cow—you can turn your dog into anything this time of year.

With just a tiny bit of creativity, you can also make your own costume for your dog. Here are some ideas to do it yourself:

- Think about a costume that fits your dog's personality. Some dogs look perfect in an angel costume, while others seem to fit devil outfit to a tee.
- Dress in a theme with your dog. Maybe you and

A Word About Costumes and Safety

Be sure that your dog's Halloween costume is comfortable. He won't have a good time if he can't move freely. Also, be sure he has clear vision. No masks for dogs! It's scary to a dog when he can't see.

Know Where Your Emergency Veterinary Hospital Is Located

If an emergency happens on a holiday, chances are your veterinary office will refer you to a nearby emergency veterinary clinic. These clinics can offer excellent care. They are often staffed with veterinarians with specialized training in emergency and trauma medicine. Before the holidays start, find the location of the emergency clinic and make a practice drive-by. That will ensure you aren't losing valuable time during an emergency trying to locate where you are going.

your significant other can don fake fur tunics and go as Fred and Wilma Flintstone. Put your Shih Tzu in her own leopard print tunic, tie a plastic bone into her topknot—and you've got Pebbles.

- Think about dog themes, too. Maybe you have a little male scruffy terrier mix, and your friend has an Afghan Hound. Your little guy just needs a vest and a peace necklace to be Sonny Bono (hey, he already has the chest hair!) and a long black wig and some sequins turns the Afghan into Cher.

- Another good choice: Dress your dogs as bride and groom. A simple veil and a white tunic for your girl and a tuxedo costume for your boy, and you've got costumed bliss. One friend who did this even made a garter for her girl dog's thigh.

- Some dogs just love to wear costumes and seem meant to wear them. Take Pugs for example. They seem made to wear anything fun you can find. Put your Pug in a pink

Little dogs love tricks and treats—just make sure his Halloween costume is safe and fits properly.

tutu, and it's funny—always.

- Every Dachshund makes an appropriate hot dog on Halloween (just add buns).
- Every diva knows a simple tiara is always appropriate (Halloween or not!).

Howl-O-Ween Party!

Invite your dog's little buddies over for a bash! Play games like "bobbing for hotdogs" (instead of bobbing for apples) and "catch the corn" (which dog can catch the most pieces of unbuttered popcorn in a minute). Have a costume contest. Hold a "Best Trick" contest (the winner earns a treat!). Ask everyone to bring cookies made for dogs, and don't forget some tasty snacks for the humans, too.

Don't spoil the fun by giving your dog something dangerous, like chocolate.

The Dangers

While Halloween can be great fun, it can also be a serious danger to your dog. Lots of dogs are frightened when hordes of small children come knocking at the door, demanding candy. Heck, it scares me a little bit, too. Here are some safety tips to keep in mind on Halloween:

Chocolate

That chocolate warning applies at Halloween, too! Also, tin foil and cellophane candy wrappers can be hazardous if your little dog swallows them.

Candles

Pumpkins with candles inside are dangerous. Your dog could knock your pumpkin over and start a fire. Use caution, and consider a battery-operated light inside your Jack-o-lantern if you have a very rambunctious little dog.

Keep Him Away from the Trick-or-Treaters

Unless your dog is an absolute social butterfly, keep him in a separate room when the trick-or-treaters come to the door. Even a kid-size Frankenstein looks pretty scary to a tiny dog.

Prevent Door Dashing

Have a system to prevent door dashing. Whether you have a dog who's frightened, or one who wants to follow the kids, Halloween is a big night for dogs escaping from home. Leave your dog in a separate room or hold him in your arms (if he's very social). Don't give him the option of dashing out the door.

Christmas

Christmas is a magical time—especially when you've got a little dog to remind how precious life truly is.

The Fun

Here are some ways to have fun with your little dog at Christmastime:

P-R-E-S-E-N-T-S!

Shopping for your dog is just as much fun as shopping for a child. There are toys, outfits, and practical gifts to buy. There are dog stockings to fill. Children may grow up and lose the magic of the season, but dogs are always willing to believe that a nice man in a red suit wants to give them piles of toys! Enjoy!

Photo with Santa-Paws

Many of the larger pet supply stores offer a photo op with your dog and Santa and, most often, the proceeds go to a good cause. And, you'll end up with the perfect Christmas card to send your friends next year.

The Outfits!

Forget the reindeer antlers—they're too hard to keep on (they look sort of like bat ears on a small dog, anyway). Think plush Santa hats or cute elf costumes. Fabulous holiday collars are available, some with beads or jingle bells. Don't forget the holiday-themed scarves and sweaters and the T-shirts that read, "I Believe!" and others that proclaim, "Bah! Humbug!" Or, if you want to go simple, a pretty red leash can put you in the holiday mood.

Giving Back

This might be a good year to spread some extra holiday cheer with your dog. If he's a social, well-mannered dog, you might want to learn about becoming certified as a therapy dog team. Therapy Dogs International (www.tdi-dog.org) or The Delta Society (www.deltasociety.org) can help you get started.

Remember That Family Is What You Make It

For a lot of people, Christmas is a bit of a blue time. Maybe you've experienced the break-up of a marriage or relationship in the past year. Possibly, your childhood wasn't a lot like *The Brady Bunch*, and the holidays bring back sad memories. Maybe Christmas just doesn't meet the hype that it receives from all the commercials.

Your dog is a reminder that you are never really alone. Family is what we make it, and so are the holidays. You might spend this time finding a separate peace with your relatives, or volunteer to help others

I hope Santa brings me that chew toy I've always wanted…

in need, or create a new community with friends. No matter how you spend the holidays, always remember you're not coming home to an empty house as long as you have your little dog. He's your little buddy who lives every waking moment for the joy of seeing your face. How can that help but be a good thing?

Enjoy the friends you've made through your dogs. The last two Christmases, I spent time with my brothers and sisters and other friends, but also spent part of

Remember Homeless Pets

The holidays are traditionally a time of sharing what we have with others who are in need. Don't forget to give a portion of your holiday giving to animals who need your help. The dogs in the shelters need your help desperately, so if you can, make a financial donation, or even better, donate your time. Your talents just might help other dogs find a home that's as magnificent as yours is for your dog.

This book is about dog beauty and style. Nothing is more beautiful or stylish than giving a helping hand to anyone (two-legged or four-legged) who's in need.

Christmas day with friends I'd made through my dogs. Your dog can bring you a community of friendship—enjoy that gift.

The Dangers

The last thing you want on Christmas is to spend the day in the emergency clinic with your little dog! Here are some holiday safety reminders to make sure that doesn't happen:

Christmas Trees

The Christmas Tree can be a hazard for small dogs. This is above and beyond the bizarre fact that we bring a tree into the living room and expect our male dogs not to do what seems natural to them!

Know your dog, and look at the tree accordingly. My dog Radar would never dream of bothering the tree once I say, "Leave it." My Pogo thinks that "Leave it" is a command that expires about every 20 seconds, and certainly doesn't apply when I'm not in the room. So, before Pogo came to the house, Christmas trees were easy. Since then, they've been challenging.

If you have an adventurous dog like my Pogo, remember:

- No glass ornaments, at least on the lower branches. When dogs are batting at ornaments, you don't want ones that can fall and break.
- No tinsel. It is indigestible, and if it gets caught in your dog's intestinal tract, you're on your way to the emergency clinic for some serious surgery.
- No food on the tree. That means no strings of popcorn (Pogo would definitely eat the popcorn, and the string would end up tangled in his tummy—yet another trip to the emergency clinic.) It also means no candy canes, since you never know what will strike a dog's fancy. It means no cute little dog treat ornaments. The dog who turns up his nose at dog treats will climb a tree to get a lacquered, painted dog treat. I don't know why, but it's true.
- No preservatives in the tree water. If you have a fresh tree, keep it well watered, but don't add those packets of preservatives to the water.
- No presents under the tree. Ribbons, paper, and boxes will be shredded if you turn your head and blink.
- Do separate the tree from the dog. Put the tree in a room that you declare off-limits to the dog unless you're there to supervise. Or, if you have a small tree, put it on a tall table so that your dog can't reach. I've resorted to putting my tree behind an exercise pen—those portable little fences that most people use to keep their dogs confined. (I decided I'd rather confine the tree than the dog.)

Will your dog ever outgrow this behavior? Maybe. A lot of boisterous puppies become very mellow adults. However, Pogo is 5, and this year I'm thinking about following a friend's advice and hanging the tree from the ceiling. Some dogs, like some people, just never grow up.

Beware of the Usual Holiday "Don'ts"

Christmas is like a holiday on steroids. Most of the "don'ts" we've discussed for other holidays apply here as well. Here's a quick reminder:

- Be sure that your dog doesn't get too much rich "people" food. This applies to any day, but no holiday has as much rich food as Christmas does.
- Make sure your dog can't dash out a door when company comes. You are likely to have more company in December than during the rest of the year combined.
- Substances like chocolate, alcohol, and caffeine are dangerous year-round, but are more likely to be in the house at Christmastime.
- Candles are always a worry. Some Christmas decorations include lighted candles

next to dry fir arrangements—just don't do it!

Keep a careful eye on your dog and his environment. Make sure that he can't get in trouble. Love him, protect him, guard him. Make sure he stays safe through the holidays.

Hanukkah

The "Festival of Lights" can be a fun time to include your dog in holiday festivities.

The Fun

There are "chewish" toys of every description, including a singing dreidel, tennis balls in the silver and blue Hanukkah colors, plush squeaky toys in the shape of bones that say "Kosher," a squeaky bear with a Star of David on its belly, and boxed Hanukkah latkes and applesauce bark bars, just to name a few of the available products.

You can celebrate the "Festival of Lights" with your little dog.

You can put the neighbor's dog's Santa hat to shame with Flytes of Fancy's (www.flytesoffancy.com) Hanukkah yarmulkes and tallis shawls, which include sizes for little dogs.

The Dangers

- The most important Hanukkah ritual is lighting the menorah. If you have a curious little dog, you'll want to supervise him while the candles are lit, to avoid accidents.
- It is traditional to eat foods fried in oil during Hanukkah. Some common foods are potato latkes and "sufganiot" (jelly doughnuts). For your little dog's health, avoid giving him any of the rich holiday food you celebrate with

New Year's Eve

When you think of New Year's Eve, you probably think of fun parties, noise, and libations. However, your little dog's idea of a perfect New Year's Eve is snuggling with you on the couch and watching the ball fall on Times Square on the television. No matter how you decide to celebrate, it is a great time to make some resolutions for the year ahead with your dog.

Make a New Year's resolution to take care of your little dog and yourself!

- I promise we'll get your weight where it belongs. In a recent study by Purina, thinner dogs lived an average of more than 2 years longer that slightly chubby ones. You want your dog with you for as many years as possible, so talk to his vet about a sensible weight loss plan.

- I promise you'll get vigorous exercise at least five times a week. That's pretty easy to do with your little dog, since it might mean just chasing his favorite toy across the living room floor for 20 minutes at a time. Walking, for most little dogs, is the ideal exercise.

- I promise you an annual physical check-up. Just do it—just one appointment a year with your vet can save your little dog's life.

- I promise to give you social time with other dogs. While a fraction of dogs don't enjoy the company of other dogs, most love to play and just hang out with other dogs. Find a play group (or start one) of other nicely behaved small dogs. Your dog will love you for it.

- I promise to take as good care of myself as I take care of you. Your dog needs for you to be healthy and long-lived, just like you want him to be. So, go get your own annual check-ups.

Check with your own doctor about a diet and exercise plan. Step one might be a long, lovely walk with your favorite dog on New Year's morning.

And that will start a whole new season in your life with your dog.

Stress Less

Do you spell "holiday" S-T-R-E-S-S?

The odds are you're spending half of December frantically shopping, wrapping presents, baking cookies, and maybe even still decorating the house. For lots of people, the holiday season is also a time when the job requires overtime hours.

As the stress piles up, imagine what you seem like to your dog. The gentle, patient person who your animal loves has suddenly morphed into a frazzled, edgy, worried jangle of nerves. Your dog will pick up on your stress, and he may be likely to bark more, turn a deaf ear to commands, and chew.

Try these stress-reducing tips to make the yuletide a little brighter:

Take a Break

Deep in your heart, you know you can accomplish more if you relax. Just 15 or 20 minutes of happy time with your pet will make all of you feel better.

A simple walk can help both you and your dog deal with holiday stress. During that walk, the two of you can renew your bond. You'll be on friendship time, not holiday time. When you come back into the house, your dog won't care if your house isn't picture perfect, and the break will remind you that sharing time with the creatures you love is part of what makes a house a home.

If you don't have 20 minutes at the moment, take 1 minute. Give your little dog a (healthy) treat. Scratch him behind the ears. Take a mini-break, and it will do wonders for your stress level.

Don't let stress get the best of you during the holiday season.

Take Your Dog with You

If you're shopping for an animal or an animal-lover, remember that most pet supply stores and boutiques welcome on-leash dogs. Your furry family member can help you pick the perfect gift.

Many stores with human merchandise are pet-friendly, too. Stores in big cities are likely to be pet friendly, and more and more stores in smaller communities are jumping on the "petwagon," too. It can't hurt to ask if your on-leash little dog can come with you. Of course, it's important to be respectful when you enter a store with your pet. Obey the cardinal rule in doggie retail etiquette: Your dog pees on it, you buy it.

It comes down to this—if you feel stressed, your pet probably does, too. If you take care of your animals' needs, you'll both feel better. You and your calmer, happier pet just might find that you have the merriest holiday season yet.

Dogs in Your Wedding? Say "I Do!"

Your dog is your friend, your family member, and your confidant. If you happen to meet the right dog-loving human to share your life with, you might want to include your dog in your wedding plans. Your dog as ring-bearer, or even "best dog"? It's more common than you might imagine. It makes a bride wonder whether to consult Emily Post or Barbara Woodhouse. Should you buy an etiquette book or an obedience manual?

Here are some thoughts on wedding "petiquette" from people who have had successful (or at the very least entertaining) dog-friendly weddings:

Want your Bichon as your "best dog"? With some careful planning, you little dog can be part of your big day.

Check Out Locations Ahead of Time

Not all parks, gardens, and chapels welcome dogs—even small, well-trained ones. If they do, you'll still want to consider whether it's a good place for your four-legged family member. Be sure there's a quiet, safe place for your animal to rest if he's feeling stressed. Look for potential hazards on the site. Ask about pesticides and toxic plants.

Planners, Preachers, and Chaperones

When you're hiring people who will work on the wedding, be sure that they are comfortable with your dog. Don't select a wedding planner who seems cold to your Chihuahua, and don't hire a preacher who turns up his nose at your Pomeranian.

The bride isn't the only one who will need attendants at this wedding. Make sure someone is in charge of your dog—making sure he's comfortable, safe, and under control. If you only have one dog at the wedding, maybe a reliable friend can be the puppy chaperone. If you have a pack of pooches, hire a doggie day care provider to supervise.

Keep Your Sense of Humor

Dogs are often asked to be ring bearers or flower-dogs. Sometimes, a sense of humor is as important as training. Dogs, like children, are unpredictable. The stress and excitement—or maybe just the sight of a favorite friend—can undo all your careful planning. Don't ask your dog to do a job he can't do, and don't be upset if he gets a little creative on your wedding day. The dogs' antics will be another story to tell for decades to come.

The Flowers

Flowers and weddings go together like, well, like love and marriage. That's true for dog-friendly weddings, too. Still, you'll have to worry about some things if your doggie flower girl will potentially eat the flowers.

Ask your florist if any of the flowers are toxic. For example, lilies, daffodils, and hydrangeas can all cause serious problems if your flower-dog swallows them.

Flowers can make your dog look festive for the occasion. Often, the dog's collar is decorated with flowers and ribbons that match the bridal bouquet.

Just secure them tightly and make sure they are nontoxic to dogs.

Party Hearty!

Are you and your dog all dressed up with no place to go? Then you'd better both put on your boots and plan to have some fun. You can find endless things to do with your dog while you meet people at the same time. Here are a few ideas:

- Doggy dashes. Many shelters have runs and walks to support their operations. Usually, dogs are welcome and even encouraged to come. You and your dog can put on your sweats, have a good time, and meet some nice people, all while supporting a good cause.

- Fur balls. Lots of organizations have fundraising parties celebrating and supporting their good work. Go to one and dance! Don't have a date? Often, well-behaved dogs are very welcome as your escort. Just put him in a black tie, since he's already wearing tails.

- Small dog play days. Join an Internet chat group for your breed, and you might find that there's a local play group just for your breed. It's a lot of fun to see all the little guys playing together. If that doesn't work, ask a local doggie day care to organize a playgroup for small dogs.

- Play dates. If you've met some nice dogs at day care or in the park, invite them and their owners for a play date at your house.

- Dog cookie exchange. Lots of neighbors have cookie exchanges at Christmas, where each household makes extra batches of their favorite cookies and shares them with each other. Do the same, except make it dog biscuits. Who can resist the smell of warm liver biscotti baking in the oven?

Little dogs may want to party all the time, but they still need their beauty sleep!

Chapter 16

When My Dog is Old She Shall Wear Purple: Senior Care

Aging isn't what it used to be. With people taking better and better care of themselves, and living much longer than we did just decades ago, senior care has become serious business. This trend has also spilled over to our four-legged family members.

It reminds me of the poem that that opens:
When I am an old women I shall wear purple
With a red hat which doesn't go, and doesn't suit me.

It's a gently worded but passionate declaration of the joys of aging—how to enjoy our own eccentricities and celebrate ourselves as we age. The poem has spawned the Red Hat Society, where women "of a certain age" don red hats and purple clothing and go out and have a good time.

Your older dog deserves the same sense of joy that the poem embraces. Our small dogs usually live very long and healthy lives, compared to larger ones. In fact, at age 14 a dog of under 20 pounds (9 kg) is considered equivalent to a 72-year-old human. A giant-sized breed at 14 would be equivalent to a person who's 108.

You can make certain changes to help your older little dog comfortable.

A lady doesn't leave the house without her head covered.

Most of all, remember to enjoy your older dog (and think about buying her a red hat!).

Grooming Your Older Dog

Your dog's skin and bones can become more sensitive with age. Often, loving humans groom their older dogs much less than when they were younger, simply because their dog seems uncomfortable. This is a big mistake. Mats hurt at any age, and they hurt more when a dog is older. Long toenails hurt little feet, and the pain is intensified for ancient little feet.

Groom your oldster every day, so that the hair is so well-brushed that you never face a mat. Keep the toenails trimmed every couple of weeks, taking off tiny little snips. Touch your dog every day, looking for lumps and bumps. Cancer is the

Help for Hearing Loss

To learn more about helping your dog learn to cope with hearing loss, check out the Deaf Dog Education Action Fund (DEAF) web site at www.deafdogs.org.

number one cause of death among older dogs, so look early for any signs of the disease.

Deafness and Blindness

Just as humans often lose all or part of their hearing and sight as they age, so do dogs. Happily, dogs adjust to those changes very well. In fact, it's not unusual for old dogs to lose most of their sight or hearing before their humans even notice that something is awry.

With just a little bit of help from you, your dog can manage these changes just fine. It's not like he has to go foraging for his own food in the wilderness, right?

For Deaf Dogs

Communicate with your dog visually. Create a large, easily noticed hand signal for "come" (for my dog, Goldie, it's a big wave of my arm). Teach your hand signal for "come" just like you train a hearing dog to respond to a verbal command. When the dog is near you, hold a treat in your hand, wave, and when the dog comes, give him the treat. Repeat from a bit farther away, until the dog realizes that, when you wave your arm, there's a treat waiting with his name on it! Reinforce with treats every time you can, so the dog is very motivated to come when you wave.

For Blind Dogs

As all baby boomers with glasses will attest, it's normal for vision to get less acute as we grow older. In addition to regular vision reduction, some diseases, such as cataracts and progressive retinal atrophy, can cause your dog to become mostly or completely blind.

Because our dogs are so tuned into us, it can be hard to notice that they've lost

Help for Blind Dogs

For excellent resources on blind dogs, check out Caroline D. Levin's book, *Living with Blind Dogs* and her video/DVD *New Skills for Blind Dogs*. There are great ideas for training and for making your home easy for a blind dog to navigate. To learn more about Levin's books, go to www.petcarebooks.com.

Goldie at Fourteen

While I was writing this book, my little Papillon Goldie celebrated her fourteenth birthday. Goldie's face once was a brilliant copper color punctuated with bright white markings; now her features are softened by shades of muted gray. She's always had the most magnificent little-dog smile, although she's now missing a tooth in front. Her eyes are still lined by dark black markings, making her look a little bit like Bette Davis in her older years, a former glamour girl wearing too much make-up.

But to me, Goldie's face is more beautiful than it's ever been. This birthday is a reminder of just how precious every day is with my old dog.

When I've told my friends that Goldie turned 14, every single one has responded with a sad, "Ohhhhhh." I'm tempted to do what one of my sisters-in-law did—for the last several years of her dog Lizzie's life, she told everyone that little Lizzie was 8. No one gives a sad, "Ohhhhhh" when you say a dog is 8. But rather than lie about Goldie's age, I'm going to try to view her senior years the same way she does. Goldie doesn't fear age; she just lives her life with joy every day.

So, I think of ways to amuse Goldie. She's quite deaf now, so I've taught her a hand signal for come, and she comes running to me with the same joy she did when she heard my voice. I regularly give her Tellington TTouch, a kind of therapeutic touch that she particularly enjoys. I remind myself to laugh and play and enjoy Goldie's golden years and not allow my own fears to get in the way of our fun.

Old dogs offer so much wisdom, dignity, and even humor. Just like my Goldie, every dog's smile just gets sweeter with age.

much of their vision. One friend of mine realized that things were different when she was in her yard. The door was open, so that her dog could go inside and out as he pleased. Instead, Sparky was barking at the open doorway, asking to be let out. He thought the screen door was in place! She showed her dog that the door was open, and he happily came out and helped her to garden. Remember to be patient with your old dog, like my friend was. It's very possible that they just aren't seeing or hearing what you expect them to.

Canine Cognitive Dysfunction

Canine cognitive dysfunction is a canine illness much like Alzheimer's disease in people. Dogs who have the disease can lose their housebreaking skills, get lost even in the living room, and stop recognizing the people in their lives. Medication can help, so if you see any symptoms of forgetfulness in your little dog, talk with your veterinarian.

Meanwhile, dogs, like people, are most likely to do well if they get mental and physical stimulation. Take your dog for walks. Enroll your oldster in a tricks class. Play games together. Have fun—you'll both be healthier if you do!

Dental Disease

Dental disease can seriously affect your dog's overall health. The bacteria from plaque can damage your dog's heart, kidney, and liver. Dental problems are much more common in older dogs than in younger ones. Keep up brushing your dog's teeth as he ages—it's more important than ever to prevent dental disease.

Senior dogs still need exercise—just keep an eye out for signs of achy joints.

Exercising Your Senior

Older dogs, like older people, benefit from exercise—in moderation. Older dogs who get regular exercise generally live longer lives and are less likely to suffer from canine cognitive dysfunction.

> ### Dog Poetry
> My little old dog:
> A heartbeat at my feet.
> —Edith Wharton

Still, you need to keep a careful eye on your older guy when he exercises. He might need slower or shorter walks than he once did. If he's got achy joints, talk with your veterinarian. There are a range of therapies available to him, from gentle pain relieving drugs to acupuncture, that might help him enjoy his exercise more.

Senior Dog Health Checklist

Most senior dogs should have twice-yearly veterinary check-ups, rather than annual visits. Make sure to see your veterinarian if you notice any of the following in your little dog:

- Weight loss
- Change in water consumption or urination
- Changes in mobility
- Deterioration of mental condition
- Bad breath (a sign that your dog needs dental work)
- Lumps and bumps
- Discuss vaccines with your veterinarian. Because some dogs can have a bad reaction to vaccines, you may decide that booster vaccines for an older dog aren't worth the risk they pose.

Aging divas know how to dress for drama— remember to have fun with your senior dog.

Final Thoughts on Little-Dog Beauty and Style

The love between a human and a dog is endlessly beautiful. It doesn't matter whether you have a dog who was rescued from a life of misery or a champion show dog—in your eyes, your little dog is one of the most perfect creations on earth.

Maybe you pamper him with real jewels. Maybe you carefully make your own velvet leash for just a couple of dollars. Perhaps you have flown together to Paris, or maybe you don't go farther from home than a walk in the park. To your dog, it doesn't matter—as long as you are together, it's all equally joyful for him.

Look into your dog's eyes, and you'll see love reflected back. And, I'm sure when he sees himself in your eyes, he sees that love returned.

Nothing in the world is more fashionable or more stylish than the love you two share. Enjoy every precious moment you have together.

Resources

Organizations

Academy of Veterinary Homeopathy (AVH)
P.O. Box 9280
Wilmington, DE 19809
Telephone: (866) 652-1590
Fax: (866) 652-1590
E-mail: office@TheAVH.org
www.theavh.org

American Holistic Veterinary Medical Association (AHVMA)
2218 Old Emmorton Road
Bel Air, MD 21015
Telephone: (410) 569-0795
Fax: (410) 569-2346
E-mail: office@ahvma.org
www.ahvma.org

American Humane Association (AHA)
63 Inverness Drive East
Englewood, CO 80112
Telephone: (303) 792-9900
Fax: 792-5333
www.americanhumane.org

American Kennel Club (AKC)
5580 Centerview Drive
Raleigh, NC 27606
Telephone: (919) 233-9767
Fax: (919) 233-3627
E-mail: info@akc.org
www.akc.org

American Society for the Prevention of Cruelty to Animals (ASPCA)
424 E. 92nd Street
New York, NY 10128-6804
Telephone: (212) 876-7700
www.aspca.org

American Veterinary Medical Association (AVMA)
1931 North Meacham Road - Suite 100
Schaumburg, IL 60173
Telephone: (847) 925-8070
Fax: (847) 925-1329
E-mail: avmainfo@avma.org
www.avma.org

American Veterinary Chiropractic Association
442154 E 140 Road
Bluejacket, Oklahoma 74333
Telephone: (918) 784-2231
Fax: (918) 784-2675
E-mail: amvetchiro@aol.com
www.animalchiropractic.org

ASPCA Animal Poison Control Center
1717 South Philo Road, Suite 36
Urbana, IL 61802
Telephone: (888) 426-4435
www.aspca.org

Association of Pet Dog Trainers (APDT)
150 Executive Center Drive Box 35
Greenville, SC 29615
Telephone: (800) PET-DOGS
Fax: (864) 331-0767
E-mail: information@apdt.com
www.apdt.com

Canadian Kennel Club (CKC)
89 Skyway Avenue, Suite 100
Etobicoke, Ontario M9W 6R4
Telephone: (416) 675-5511
Fax: (416) 675-6506
E-mail: information@ckc.ca
www.ckc.ca

Deaf Dog Education Action Fund
P.O. Box 2840
Oneco, FL 34264-2840
www.deafdogs.org

Delta Society
875 124th Ave NE, Suite 101
Bellevue, WA 98005
Telephone: (425) 226-7357
Fax: (425) 235-1076
E-mail: info@deltasociety.org
www.deltasociety.org

Federation Cynologique Internationale (FCI)
Secretariat General de la FCI
Place Albert 1er, 13
B - 6530 Thuin
Belqique
www.fci.be

The Humane Society of the United States (HSUS)
2100 L Street, NW
Washington DC 20037
Telephone: (202) 452-1100
www.hsus.org

International Agility Link (IAL)
Global Administrator: Steve Drinkwater
E-mail: yunde@powerup.au
www.agilityclick.com/~ial

International Veterinary Acupuncture Society
P.O. Box 271395
Ft. Collins, CO 80527-1395
Telephone: (970) 266-0666
Fax: (970) 266-0777
www.ivas.org

The Kennel Club
1 Clarges Street
London
W1J 8AB
Telephone: 0870 606 6750
Fax: 0207 518 1058
www.the-kennel-club.org.uk

National Association of Professional Pet Sitters
15000 Commerce Parkway, Suite C
Mt. Laurel, NJ 08054
Telephone: (800) 296-PETS
Fax: (856) 439-0525
E-mail: napps@ahint.com
www.petsitters.org

North American Dog Agility Council
11522 South Hwy 3
Cataldo, ID 83810
www.nadac.com

Northwest School of Animal Massage
P.O. Box 670
Fall City. WA 98024
Telephone: (877) 836-3703
Fax: (425) 222-4573
www.nwsam.com.

Pet Sitters International
201 East King Street
King, NC 27021-9161
Telephone: (336) 983-9222
Fax: (336) 983-5266
E-mail: info@petsit.com
www.petsit.com

Royal Society for the Prevention of Cruelty to Animals (RSPCA)
Telephone: 0870 3335 999
Fax: 0870 7530 284
www.rspca.org.uk

Therapy Dogs International (TDI)
88 Bartley Road
Flanders, NJ 07836
Telephone: (973) 252-9800
Fax: (973) 252-7171
E-mail: tdi@gti.net
www.tdi-dog.org

United Kennel Club (UKC)
100 E. Kilgore Road
Kalamazoo, MI 49002-5584
Telephone: (269) 343-9020
Fax: (269) 343-7037
E-mail: pbickell@ukcdogs.com
www.ukcdogs.com

United States Dog Agility Association
P.O. Box 850955
Richardson, TX 75085-0955
Telephone: (972) 487-2200
www.usdaa.com

Publications
Books

Levin, Caroline D., *Blind Dog Stories: Tales of Triumph, Humor and Heroism,* Lantern Publications, 1999.

Levin, Caroline D., *Living With Blind Dogs: A Resource Book and Training Guide for the Owners of Blind and Low Vision Dogs,* Lantern Publications, 2003.

Traveling with Your Pet: The AAA PetBook, AAA Publications, 2001.

Magazines

AKC Family Dog
American Kennel Club
260 Madison Avenue
New York, NY 10016
Telephone: (800) 490-5675
E-mail: familydog@akc.org
www.akc.org/pubs/familydog

AKC Gazette
American Kennel Club
260 Madison Avenue
New York, NY 10016
Telephone: (800) 533-7323
E-mail: gazette@akc.org
www.akc.org/pubs/gazette

Dog & Kennel
Pet Publishing, Inc.
7-L Dundas Circle
Greensboro, NC 27407
Telephone: (336) 292-4272
Fax: (336) 292-4272
E-mail: info@petpublishing.com
www.dogandkennel.com

Dog Fancy
Subscription Department
P.O. Box 53264
Boulder, CO 80322-3264
Telephone: (800) 365-4421
E-mail: barkback@dogfancy.com
www.dogfancy.com

Dogs Monthly
Ascot House
High Street, Ascot,
Berkshire SL5 7JG
United Kingdom
Telephone: 0870 730 8433
Fax: 0870 730 8431
E-mail: admin@rtc-associates.freeserve.co.uk
www.corsini.co.uk/dogsmonthly

Websites

Barking Baby
www.barkingbaby.com
Apparel and accessories for the fashionable dog.

Boomerang Tags
www.boomerangtags.com
High-quality ID tags for your dog.

Dinky Dawg Shoppe
www.dinkydawg.com
Handmade apparel that is customized for a perfect fit for your toy dog.

Dog.com
www.dog.com
The dog's outfitter.

Doggles
www.doggles.com
Protective eyewear for dogs.

Doggy Duds
www.doggyduds.com
Dog costumes for everyday wear, special occasions, and holidays.

Fiber Trends
www.fibertrends.com
Over 200 designs and products for
knitters and crocheters.

Flytes of Fancy
www.flytesoffancy.com
Offers a selection of pet costumes and
accessories to suit almost any occasion.

Good Dogma
www.gooddogma.com
Aromatherapy and furnishings for dogs
and their homes.

In the Company of Dogs
www.inthecompanyofdogs.com
Accessories and all things dog.

Just Pet Strollers
www.justpetstrollers.com
Strollers made just for dogs.

K9 Top Coat
www.k9topcoat.com
Functional, comfortable, durable and
fashionable garments for your dog.

Karp Styles
www.karpstyles.com
Crochet patterns and knitting pattern
books and supplies.

Kings Jewelers Fancy Bones Jewelry
www.fancybones.com
An exclusive line of pet ID tags and dog
jewelry for people and pets.

Linda Tellington-Jones' TTOUCH
www.tteam-ttouch.com
Learn how Tellington TTouch can help
you create a more wonderful partnership
with your horse, dog, cat, bird, bunny or
another animal companion.

Paw Printz Pet Boutique
www.pawprintzpetboutique.com
Specializing in canine couture.

Pets Welcome
www.petswelcome.com
The internet's largest pet/travel resource,
with listings for over 25,000 hotels,
B&Bs, ski resorts, campgrounds, and
beaches that are pet-friendly.

Purina
www.purina.com
For information and health studies on
weight loss.

Ruff Ruff & Meow
www.ruffruffandmeow.com
Fun and funky dog clothes, including T-
shirts, tank tops, and doggie accessories.

Ruff Wear
www.ruffwear.com
Boots and other safe, innovative gear for
dogs on the go.

ThreadDog
www.threaddog.com
Stylish and functional collars for the
active small dog.

William Secord Gallery
www.dogpainting.com
Specializes in the exhibition and sale of
fine nineteenth and twentieth century
dog paintings, works on paper, bronzes,
and books—all with the dog as their
subject matter.

Index

Note: numbers in boldface denote captions

Dedication

For Goldie, Radar and Pogo—three little Papillons with a natural sense of style.

Acknowledgements

I owe an enormous debt of gratitude to Suzanne Hein, owner of LexiDog Boutique & Social Club, for giving me the best ideas in this book. She's hip, she's urban, she is the purveyor of the Next Big Thing. She was kind and generous with her help-and she has the hippest dog spot in Portland.

I am so grateful to TFH for asking me to write this book. Heather Russell-Revesz is every writer's dream editor: smart, kind, and patient. Heather, you've been a goddess! And thanks to Mary Ann Kahn for turning my prose into colorful images that are a treat for the senses.

Many people gave me ideas to help with this book, for which I am eternally grateful. Special thanks to Lisa Keppinger, Lisa Harper, and Robin Thompson for being there when I needed them.

My friends have been patient with my absence as I holed up to write. Special thanks to two terrific cheerleaders, Dale De Roest and Leah Atwood, who made it easier. Thanks to Joel Gavriele-Gold for reminding me that there is always the next project, and for Arlie Hutchens who dropped everything to help when I let the rest of my life get behind!

Photo Credits

Photos on pages 36, 169 courtesy of Jill Arnel

Photos on pages 4, 15, 28 courtesy of barkingbaby.com

Photos on pages 5, 10, 11, 12, 16, 18, 23, 40, 42, 46, 49, 54, 56, 80, 85, 88, 108, 115, 116, 118, 122, 126, 130, 135, 140, 148, 150, 153, 154, 155, 158, 160, 163, 164, 166, 171, 172, 174, 176, 180 courtesy of Paulette Braun

Photos on pages 9, 24, 60 courtesy of dinkydawg.com

Photos on pages 21, 27, 34, 38, 58, 63, 65, 67, 69, 70, 72, 73, 75, 76, 83, 84, 86, 90, 91, 92, 96, 98, 99, 101, 102, 104, 106, 110, 113, 120, 123, 124, 127, 128, 132, 134, 136, 138, 142, 143, 145, 146, 149, 179 courtesy of Isabelle Francais

Photo on page 26 courtesy of K9TopCoat.com

Photos on pages 30, 50, 55 courtesy of LexiDog Boutique & Social Club

Photo on page 170 courtesy of Robert Pearcy

Photos on pages 14, 51 courtesy of ruffruffandmeow.com

Photo on page 178 courtesy of Sue Waddington

Front and back cover photos courtesy of Paulette Braun